TRUE HISTORY

THE LEGACY OF JIM CROW

TRUE HISTORY

THE LEGACY OF JIM CROW

BY CLARENCE A. HAYNES

SERIES CREATED BY JENNIFER SABIN

PENGUIN WORKSHOP

For educators and young people around the world—CAH

PENGUIN WORKSHOP
An imprint of Penguin Random House LLC, New York

First published in the United States of America by Penguin Workshop,
an imprint of Penguin Random House LLC, New York, 2022

Photo insert credits: Joint Resolution to Abolish Slavery, the Thirteenth Amendment: Library of Congress Prints and Photographs Division; The Statue of Liberty: TriggerPhoto/iStock/Getty Images; Nineteenth-Century African American Leaders: Library of Congress Prints and Photographs Division; NAACP Flag flies in 1920: Library of Congress Prints and Photographs Division; March on Washington, 1963: (Protestors) National Archives photo no. 542044, (Marchers) National Archives photo no. 542045; Bayard Rustin: Library of Congress Prints and Photographs Division; Toni Morrison: Library of Congress Prints and Photographs Division; Black Lives Matter Memorial: Joan Shaffer, [Photographs of the Black Lives Matter memorial and protest signs in Washington, DC], 2020, Library of Congress, Prints & Photographs Division, LC-DIG-ppbd-01198

Visit us online at penguinrandomhouse.com.

Library of Congress Cataloging-in-Publication Data is available.

Manufactured in Canada

ISBN 9780593385999 10 9 8 7 6 5 4 3 2 1 FRI

CONTENTS

FOREWORD
A NOTE FROM JENNIFER SABIN, THE CREATOR OF TRUE HISTORY

As a radio and television news writer and editor for seventeen years, I was used to a certain pace of work. Broadcast newsrooms are like hospitals: The day can hum along quietly, efficiently—until out of nowhere, a bomb goes off, a plane crashes, or a fire wreaks havoc on a community, and suddenly, you're moving at one hundred miles per hour. The difference, of course, is that reporting the news isn't usually a matter of life or death (unless you're reporting from a war zone).

There is an addictive quality to journalism—waiting or searching for the next story; wondering when the adrenaline rush will come, kicking the newsroom into high gear. In broadcasting, those stories can come fast and furiously, and there isn't always an opportunity to delve into a subject. Thirty seconds might be all you have to report on the deadly tornado that ripped through a small town.

Writing about history forces you to move in the other direction, combing through the lives of the newsmakers of the past and the work of the historians who have tried to make sense of it all. It's a slower pace that requires patience. The mountain of material can be daunting—enormous biographies, detailed historical accounts, online essays, and the letters and financial accounts of an important figure. It's another kind of rush: the joy of uncovering some gem that makes the hours of research worth the trouble, connecting the dots in lives lived hundreds of years ago.

This series doesn't pretend to read all that material or tell every story, each biography in full—not even close. I've approached this series as a journalist, in an effort to locate and piece together some of what we miss when we're told the story of the United States of America. My goal is to point out some of the half-truths and lies we are taught as children and to present history through a more critical lens, in the narratives that are often just a footnote to the text or left out entirely, through the voices that aren't always heard when US students open their history books.

Some Americans prefer to leave those stories out of the text for good, believing that they diminish the United States and teach children to hate their country.

On the contrary, Americans can understand difficult truths about their country and still love it dearly. In the words of the great author James Baldwin, "I love America more than any other country in the world, and, exactly for this reason, I insist on the right to criticize her perpetually."

Who does it serve if we are taught myths rather than facts, if we only hear from the perspective of the oppressors and not the oppressed? If we are only told the part of the story that glorifies the nation's founding and deifies the men who led the way?

The story changes and grows, becomes fuller and more nuanced, when different voices participate. It matters who tells the story, when they tell it, and how they choose to present the facts. Textbooks often present a version of history that is sanitized for young audiences, presented to promote patriotism and American exceptionalism: The idea that the United States, as the greatest country on earth, is a force for good in the world with a unique mission to spread freedom and democracy. In that telling, stories that paint the country in a negative light are often struck from the record.

The True History series seeks to help rectify those shortcomings one subject at a time, through interviews and documentation, perspective, and context.

How does the history of Jim Crow in the United States provide context to the Black Lives Matter movement and the systemic racism that still infects our country? Does the story of the United States' first leaders reach different conclusions when women write about the Founders? (Sometimes, yes.) What happens when an Indigenous person looks back to reflect on how the history of his people in the Americas affects Native American life today? And how does the story of immigration in the United States change when we look at it from new perspectives?

With the True History series, we're looking back, but we're also looking inward at the United States' successes and systemic problems and how the past has delivered the country to the present. We're also looking ahead to how we might take the lessons of history and reorient ourselves in the present to find new ways forward.

The Legacy of Jim Crow sets out *not* to rewrite history but to present some of the existing facts that paint a more honest picture than American kids are usually taught about US history, Black history in particular. Some of that history has been omitted from the books and the lessons kids are taught; some of it has been whitewashed. But all of it must be preserved, taught, and discussed. Our hope is that in the process of learning more about that history, you will better understand the connections of the past to some of the issues facing the country today.

The murder of George Floyd on May 25, 2020, galvanized a national movement against the police brutality that plagues the United States. That event, and the Black Lives Matter protests that followed, underscored how important it is for us to learn the history of that violence and the mass incarceration that disproportionately harms and kills Black Americans.

After the 2020 election, a number of states enacted voter suppression laws designed to make it harder for certain groups of people to vote. Some critics of these laws have called them "Jim Crow 2.0." To understand why, and how harmful such laws will be to the US electoral process, it is critical to know the history of Jim Crow laws, and the history that preceded them.

The discussion of reparations for Black Americans has been gaining momentum. You might ask why. In order for Americans to have an intelligent conversation about this issue, it is crucial that they—that you—understand the history of economic policies that have purposefully harmed Black Americans and made it more difficult for them to accumulate wealth.

It is also important for you to learn the countless positive contributions that Black Americans have made to the United States and continue to make every day in spite of this difficult history. *The Legacy of Jim Crow* and the True History series aim to highlight some of these contributions.

I hope you find this book, and this series, illuminating and thought-provoking. And I hope it sparks discussion and debate in your homes and your classrooms, the kinds of conversations I always enjoyed in the newsroom.

INTRODUCTION
A NOTE FROM PROFESSOR DAVID IKARD

Ikard is a professor of African American and Diaspora Studies at Vanderbilt University.

In 1798, French military leader Napoleon Bonaparte set out to conquer and colonize Egypt. To do so, he brought along with him lots of firepower, including four hundred ships and fifty-four thousand men. What was particularly unique about his attempt at conquest was that he also brought 150 savants—including scholars, engineers, scientists, and scribes.

A colonizing "gangsta" in every sense of the word, Napoleon understood that the process of conquering a culture went far beyond physically dominating a group and forcing them to comply with your laws and values. It meant overhauling their entire culture, from academics to religion to holiday celebrations.

Though Napoleon failed to conquer Egypt, he was wildly successful in conquering Egyptian/African culture. His savants wrote impressive volumes of literature on African wildlife, religion, cooking practices, and developments in science, mathematics, and philosophy. The most gangsterest move, however, was to place European culture at the center of Egyptian/African culture. They not only rewrote the history of Egypt, but they also took credit for the innovations and advancements of the culture. The evil genius of this move was clear: teach the conquered group to think of the conquerors as organically superior and thus rightfully entitled to control the country and rule over its inhabitants. Today, we have a phrase for such a move: Columbusing.

If you've never heard this word before, the term flips the script on the romanticized narrative of how the Americas were discovered. The undisputed hero in this narrative is Christopher Columbus. As the fabled story goes, Columbus was actually in search of a commercially advantageous route to Asia, or the Indies as it was called in his day. In fact, when he landed in the present-day Bahamas, he thought he was in the Indies. The Indigenous folks he encountered were referred to as "Indians" for this very reason. Clearly you cannot "discover" a land that is already inhabited. What you can do, however, is colonize and enslave the inhabitants and rewrite the history as one of glorious discovery. So, what does this mean for those groups that were already there? For their history; for their culture; for their legacy; for their humanity? It means, in short, erasing their existence beyond how they fit into our cultural narrative of discovery. The term *Columbusing*, then, denotes the process by which one group takes credit for, or recklessly appropriates, the accomplishments of another group.

The whitewashed story of Christopher Columbus was one of many that were drilled into my head during my educational process. I was taught that historical white figures like George Washington and Thomas Jefferson were superheroes of democracy without once being informed of their status as enslavers. I was also taught that Abraham Lincoln, aka "The Great Emancipator," freed enslaved people without being told about his deeply troubling white supremacist views. I never learned, for instance, that he wanted to ship the previously enslaved Africans back to Africa because he feared that their very presence would complicate the ability to reunite whites following a bloody Civil War that claimed over seven hundred thousand lives. In all of these invented fictions masquerading as historical "truths," African Americans were always featured as minor players in America's grand narrative of democracy. Slavery—America's original sin—was regrettable, for sure, but the upside was that it "rescued" Africans from a primitive culture and existence, introduced them to Christianity (thus saving their souls from eternal damnation), and opened up new opportunities for self-improvement and self-determination.

If all the good guys in your history lessons are white and all the bad guys are Black and brown, then it's real easy to imagine yourself, and people that look like you, as inferior. That's why as a kid, I hated discussing slavery or Africa or anything that related to Black oppression. Africa was culturally backward, poor, and dirty. There was nothing of value to claim as one of its descendants. Our community internalized these white supremacist beliefs so deeply that we called each other "African booty-scratchers" and "Black Africans" as insults. Truth be told, I was guilty of weaponizing these terms as well and have the battle scars to prove it.

In stark contrast, this whitewashed history encouraged my white peers to see themselves as superior to their Black peers.

Even though by the time I was born in 1972 open celebration of white supremacy was becoming increasingly taboo, de facto segregation in practically all facets of American life was the norm. I distinctly recall witnessing my first Ku Klux Klan march when I was about ten years old. While I had no idea what I was witnessing sitting in my car with my mom as the white supremacists marched and chanted slurs, I knew that it was destructive by the sheer look of horror and disdain on my mother's face. I was later to learn that the march was sparked by a Black couple who purchased a house on the "white" side of our small, one stoplight southern town. As I recall, the intimidation tactic worked. The Black couple not only sold their house, they moved out of town.

Spanish philosopher George Santayana once noted that "Those who cannot remember the past are condemned to repeat it." Though in my forty-nine years on this earth I have witnessed tremendous strides in terms of racial progress (including the election and reelection of the first Black president and the election of the first woman and Black and South Asian vice president), I have also been alarmed by a recent resurgence of white supremacy. It should go without saying that the health of our democracy depends on our willingness as citizens to learn and grow from our past mistakes and shortcomings as a nation.

Whitewashing history, then, is not only irresponsible but dangerously so. While telling the truth of who we are and what we have done to our most vulnerable populations will certainly make some of us uncomfortable—especially those in power who have most benefited from this historical distortion—it is a necessary step toward maintaining the viability of our democracy.

To borrow from Black cultural vernacular, Clarence A. Haynes "understood the assignment" in writing *The Legacy of Jim Crow*. His goal is not only to set the record straight on the Jim Crow era, but, more importantly, to help us appreciate how far we have come since then and how far we have yet to go. However much we may like to think that social progress is inevitable and racial equality is the primary goal of our republic, there are clear signs that this is not necessarily the case for far too many Americans. Despite this reality, I remain convinced that our better angels will win out if we continue to grapple earnestly and openly with our past.

CHAPTER 1
WHAT'S BEEN HIDDEN

For those who find themselves cruising down a certain section of New York Harbor, the Statue of Liberty looms overhead. The 151-foot, world-renowned monument was erected in 1886. The name of the sculpture represents a simple idea of American freedom, yet the statue's history is layered, symbolizing a more nuanced look at society. Sculptor Frédéric-Auguste Bartholdi's preliminary sketches of the statue showed her holding a broken chain, perhaps to honor the abolition of slavery in the United States. Ultimately, the chain would be placed at the statue's feet, hard to find and partially hidden by the hem of her robes. Instead of a broken chain, Lady Liberty holds in her arm a tablet engraved in Roman numerals with the date July 4, 1776. This is when the American colonies adopted the Declaration of Independence, asserting their freedom from Great Britain with the claim "all Men are created equal."

Yet the United States has a long tradition of creating laws that have discriminated against many of its own citizens, *not* treating all people as equals. A variety of groups—women, people of color, LGBTQIA+ communities, Indigenous communities, and immigrants, for example—have faced unequal treatment over the course of US history. These laws have taken different forms over the years and have had a big impact on millions of people's lives, causing everything from unfulfilled dreams to death. These laws have impacted who can make governmental or financial or cultural decisions for the country, shaping our collective experiences. These stories have often been withheld from history books—submerged, covered up, and hidden from the public eye.

II. A Nation of Bondage

A more honest assessment of the nation's origins means looking directly at the bondage (the state of being enslaved) of generations of human beings. Slavery became part of the American economy beginning in 1619, when there was just one colony in the land that would later become the United States. A small group of African people from a region that is now known as the country of Angola were captured and brought to an unfamiliar land, with the enslaved population growing significantly over the decades. When the United States was later founded in 1776, slavery was a common practice in America and a huge driving force behind its economy. Even the so-called Founding Fathers, heralded by many for their enlightened views, had enslaved hundreds of people of African descent. In fact, during the Revolutionary War, some of the enslaved fought on the side of the British, who offered them freedom from the bondage of colonists.

The system of US slavery was fueled by greed and racism, a concept that says that people who are of African descent should be treated unequally, often terribly, because of the color of our skin. Almost one hundred years later, right before the Civil War of 1861–65, nearly four million people of African descent were enslaved in the United States. The enslaved were forced to live under codes that greatly limited their movement and took away almost all of the rights we now take for granted.

American slavery would become mainly linked to the production of cotton in the South. To pick this crop, people of African descent were forced to work in big fields of land known as plantations, now called labor camps by some. By 1860, in the Southern states that would declare independence from the North, around 32 percent of white families had enslaved Black people. The trauma of slavery can still be seen to this day in society.

A CLOSER LOOK: SLAVERY IN THE AMERICAS

The concept of slavery has existed around the world for eons. To enslave someone is to claim ownership over somebody else's life, controlling what they can do every day. Slavery was common in ancient Rome, for example, around two thousand years ago. Unlike slavery in America centuries later, it wasn't based on skin color, though most of the enslaved were considered foreigners.

The ***transatlantic slave trade*** took place from the 1500s to the 1800s, a period in which more than ten million enslaved Africans were taken to North and South America. In this system, Africans were kidnapped from their homes, chained, brought to another land on ships, and forced to work to make money for people of European descent. This system was violent and awful, a violation of human rights in terrible, countless ways. Some people were beaten so badly that they died; others had parts of their bodies cut off or were scarred forever. Women were routinely raped by the masters of plantations.

The kidnapping of all these people damaged communities in Africa, causing huge instability. At the same time, important cultural traditions managed to survive the trade and were transformed on American shores.

Slavery as a legal practice finally ended with the Thirteenth Amendment, which was passed and ratified by Congress in 1865. Yet Black communities continued to deal with other laws that discriminated against us because of the color of our skin. Some of the most harmful of these laws comprised the system of Jim Crow, a strict group of policies adopted in Southern states years after the Civil War. Jim Crow laws were created to stop Black people from having access to the same opportunities and resources as whites, helping to maintain a rigid caste system that had existed since slavery. These laws existed from the late 1800s until the 1960s. We'll talk about the system of Jim Crow at length in our next chapter.

Even though the Declaration of Independence had been created with the words "all Men are created equal," the existence of slavery in America for more than two hundred years directly contradicted this statement. Why would the Founders of the United States express this idea yet still hold so many in bondage? This small group prioritized their own economic interests and vision for America over the fate of the lives of the enslaved, a dynamic explored in *The Founders Unmasked*, another book in the True History series.

Another big question: How has this system of slavery and oppression shaped the United States to this day? We hope to help you gain answers to this question, taking you through elements of this history step-by-step.

WHAT'S THAT WORD?

Caste (say: kast) refers to the rigid divisions found in a society. In a caste system, some people are considered better than others due to categories like skin color, ethnic background, wealth, and religion. India is well known for having a caste system that lasted for thousand of years and still affects the nation. Caste systems can be found in other countries, too.

Pulitzer Prize–winning journalist and author Isabel Wilkerson has studied the concept of caste. She wrote an acclaimed 2020 book that focused on caste in America, which has helped to change discussions about race. She asserts that African Americans have long been at the bottom of the caste system in the country of their birth, which has greatly impacted how they are treated.

III. A Sprawling Web of Racism

Jim Crow was used as a title for the laws of the South that discriminated against Black people. (We will use both terms "African American" and "Black" throughout the text while keeping in mind that plenty of Black and brown people in America come from other countries. The author of this book readily identifies as Black and African American, with a family that hails from Panama and other parts of the Caribbean.) This concept of Jim Crow, of constantly placing Black people in a lower caste, has impacted many, many aspects of American life, creating what can be called systemic, or structural, racism.

WHAT DOES *THAT* MEAN?

Systemic racism, or ***structural racism***, is the process through which the beliefs and attitudes of racism become firmly fixed in a society's political, economic, and cultural institutions. Systemic racism—a core element of Jim Crow laws—leads to discrimination in areas like housing, education, criminal justice, and employment that can last for generations, affecting millions of lives.

For decades, African Americans could only live in certain areas and weren't given the same types of job opportunities as white citizens. Black people have also faced decades of discrimination within the criminal justice system, being over-policed where they live, and subjected to police brutality while receiving tougher prison sentences for committing the same crimes as their white counterparts. And Jim Crow ideas have dictated how Black people are presented in TV shows, movies, and other cultural offerings.

We will touch on these areas to help illuminate some of the social issues of our time, and to show how Jim Crow has influenced different parts of American life, forming a web of ideas and policies that have snared individuals and communities. This notion of a web will inform our approach, highlighting how acts of discrimination are connected, constantly in conversation with one another. Readers can view what we go over as brief, meditative glimpses into parts of history, meant to inspire deeper exploration.

As you've just seen with the discussion of slavery, some of the information presented in these pages will be very disturbing, detailing different types of trauma that generations of people have endured. We encourage young readers to talk about this with their teachers and other adults, to take breaks if what you're reading feels too tough. Though these stories can be shocking, we believe it's important to present elements of history that have often been hidden because they make people uncomfortable. Knowing the truth about a country's history can lead to informed awareness, making sure the horrors of the past remain in the past. And a super important note: For those whose ancestors experienced some of what we'll describe in these pages, know that no one should ever be defined solely by the trauma they've endured. Your humanity—one's joys, desires, fears, and varied interests—must be front and center. For this reason, each of the following chapters will begin with people who are artists and creators, sharing their gifts with the world as they help us understand the concept of legacy.

It's from this place we will proceed.

LET'S TALK ABOUT IT

* Why do you think the chain once held by the Statue of Liberty was placed at her feet?
* What are some lessons you've learned in school about freedom and liberty in the United States? What about on TV or social media? Where does the concept of slavery fit into what you've learned?
* How familiar are you with the concept of Jim Crow? Can you think of any specific examples of a Jim Crow law from American history?

CHAPTER 2
THE MAKINGS OF OPPRESSION

The late Nobel Prize winner Toni Morrison is world renowned for the exquisite writing found in her books. Having gotten her start as an editor, she has authored novels like *The Bluest Eye* and *Beloved*, which are taught in high schools and colleges around the country. What many people may not know is that she was born in the midwestern town of Lorain, Ohio, in 1931 in a diverse, working-class neighborhood. "Everybody was either somebody from the South or an immigrant from east Europe or from Mexico," Morrison once said about her hometown in a 2015 interview with journalist Terry Gross.

Her parents were among those who were from the South,

having both made their way north earlier in life. Her father, George, was originally from Cartersville, Georgia, and during his childhood he was deeply traumatized. He witnessed two neighbors who were Black businessmen killed on his street by an act of lynching.

Morrison's mother, Ramah, was originally from Alabama, where her family was involved in a type of farming known as sharecropping. Though she spoke of parts of her childhood in the South with sweetness, Ramah chose never to return to the land of her birth after moving to Lorain.

The experiences of Morrison and her parents touch on the realities of African American life in the twentieth century: the looming presence of a type of labor that weighed heavily on people's bodies and souls, the public murder of Black people in spaces where they should have been safe, and the movement of great numbers of people from the South, looking for opportunity and refuge. Jim Crow laws were responsible for all of these items, connecting to some of the most violent and oppressive elements of US history.

II. New Forms of Oppression

As discussed in the previous chapter, slavery fueled the US

economy for some time. Toward the end of the Civil War, the Thirteenth Amendment was adopted in December 1865, officially ending slavery in the United States. Yet this amendment also stated that someone's freedom could be taken away if they were found guilty of wrongdoing in the court of law.

A CLOSER LOOK: WHAT IS THE THIRTEENTH AMENDMENT?

When looking at the US Constitution, an ***amendment*** is a change or addition to the original document put forth in 1789. The Constitution's first ten amendments, grouped together as the **Bill of Rights**, were adopted in 1791. The Constitution has had twenty-seven amendments ratified so far.

The **Thirteenth Amendment** was passed and ratified in 1865 during **Reconstruction**. The amendment states: "Neither slavery nor involuntary servitude, except as a punishment for crime whereof the party shall have been duly convicted, shall exist within the United States, or any place subject to their jurisdiction." This means that slavery was officially over in America except when someone was convicted of a crime. Slavery could thus still exist in the country in a different form, with imprisoned people providing free labor. Scholars have pointed to the outcome of the 1871 Virginia Supreme Court case *Ruffin v. Commonwealth* as an example of this. The ruling states that someone who is a convict could indeed be seen as "a slave of the State" during the time of their sentence.

Even though slavery was declared over, many white Southerners found new ways to oppress Black citizens with different types of "Black codes," which were connected to previously established rules that the enslaved were forced to follow. Mississippi and South Carolina adopted the first codes in 1865, the same year the Civil War ended. In South Carolina, African Americans could only work as farmers or servants, though exceptions could be made if they paid a high tax. In Mississippi, Black citizens had to have written proof of having a job. They could be fined and arrested if they left their job before the terms of their contract ended. And thus, some African Americans had their freedom taken away once again right after slavery had officially ended.

Some of the codes also asserted that Black citizens

couldn't own certain types of property, and that they could be arrested for "loitering" or "vagrancy." This meant that African Americans could be jailed for simply standing around on the street and not appearing to be at work. Black people who couldn't afford their fines had to pay off the fees through forced labor, toiling at the same type of agricultural work they had to do when they were enslaved. And so began the convict leasing system, where tens of thousands of Black prisoners could be sent to farms, lumber camps, plantations, and other businesses in the South. This setup was beneficial to the former Confederate states, which were in economic ruin after the war.

Scholar Michelle Alexander described this time as the first prison boom in the United States, when the prison population grew at an enormous rate. The conditions at these convict leasing sites were extremely inhumane, leading to death for some. Black children could also be forced to work. These codes helped to keep African Americans at the bottom of the US caste system even with slavery abolished.

Another way of maintaining systemic racism was through sharecropping, which was considered a form of tenant farming. In sharecropping, which became popular in the

1870s on former plantations, a farmer would rent land and equipment from a landowner. In exchange, the landowner would receive a portion of the crop farmed by the tenant. These crops could be anything from cotton to tobacco. A fair system? Well, not really. It was easy for white landowners to arrange the system so that sharecroppers were always in debt. This system ended up binding families to the land for decades. Some even called the setup a type of debt slavery, and most sharecroppers were African American.

III. The Reconstruction Era

As former Confederate states devised new ways to oppress Black citizens, Congress passed legislation that granted more rights on paper to African Americans as part of the Reconstruction era, which was from 1865–1877. Still, these laws were biased and didn't grant full social equality to the formerly enslaved. The Civil Rights Act of 1866 stated that, going forth, Black people born in the United States would be considered full-fledged citizens. But when sponsoring the act, Congress purposely avoided granting full social rights to African Americans. In fact, lawmakers deleted specific language that would have outlawed discrimination based on skin color. This was done so that the president at the time, Andrew Johnson, would sign the law. Johnson was known for his racism, allowing former Confederate politicians to return to power and publicly declaring white supremacist beliefs that envisioned African Americans occupying a lower caste permanently.

The Fourteenth (1868) and Fifteenth Amendments (1870) would go on to protect certain citizenship rights for African Americans and establish the right to vote for Black men. (Women wouldn't be able to vote until the Nineteenth Amendment was ratified in 1920.) The Reconstruction era was a time of fresh opportunity as the Black codes were done away with, though many white politicians and regular citizens alike opposed the reforms. Black men from the South were elected to Congress, including Hiram Revels of Mississippi. In 1870, Revels became the first African American to serve in the US Senate after a special election in his state's legislature. Blanche K. Bruce was later sworn in, the first African American to serve a full term as senator, starting in 1875. Sixteen Black men served in Congress during Reconstruction and hundreds served in state legislatures, among other positions of influence.

NOW LET'S TAKE A MOMENT . . .

Congress during the Reconstruction era reached new levels of diversity, but this would be short-lived as Jim Crow was put into effect. After Blanche K. Bruce, almost one hundred years passed before another African American senator was elected to office. Congress has been made up of mostly white men throughout its history, a direct legacy of who the country's Founding Fathers were. The 117th Congress sworn in for 2021 is considered the most ethnically diverse ever, but is still disproportionately white compared to the US population, particularly when viewing the Senate.

IV. The Birth of Segregation

Even with the seeming progress made during Reconstruction, Southern states would find new ways to oppress African Americans and maintain the caste system previously established. "With the passage of the 14th and 15th Amendments, there was a shift over to Jim Crow laws, which were kind of a perpetuation of the black codes," said Dr. Connie Hassett-Walker, a scholar of criminal justice and sociology. "You don't just flip the switch and all that structural discrimination and hatred just turns off. It kept going." Those who wished to keep African Americans in a lower caste, whose vision of society was based on this oppression, needed to find new ways to do so as slavery and the Black codes were no longer available to them.

IN THE MEDIA: WHO EXACTLY WAS JIM CROW?

Jim Crow was a character created by nineteenth-century white entertainer **Thomas Dartmouth Rice** after he observed an elderly African American stable hand dancing and singing. Rice allegedly took the song he heard, apparently called "Jump Jim Crow," and performed in live shows as the title character from the late 1820s to the 1840s. To do so, he covered his face with burnt cork, appearing in a type of makeup called blackface. Rice relied on exaggerated language and gestures for his performances. Characters like Jim Crow reinforced untrue, damaging stereotypes about African Americans, fueling discrimination and violence. The character's name was eventually used to refer to the racist laws that arose after Reconstruction, continuing the harsh caste system placed upon Black people.

Though considered far less acceptable now than

in the 1800s, blackface appeared onstage and in film and TV throughout the twentieth century. Even in the 2000s, people are still having to protest instances of blackface and brownface found on social media.

Reconstruction ended in 1877 as white Southerners created what would be known as Jim Crow laws. These policies were in many ways an extension of the Black codes put into place right after the Civil War. Historians mark the 1896 Supreme Court decision *Plessy v. Ferguson* as when Jim Crow policies were given full reign. This ruling stated that "separate but equal" spaces for Black and white people were acceptable nationwide. But as history would show, separate facilities were generally *not* equal, with African Americans unable to access the same social and financial resources as whites.

Jim Crow laws expanded all across the South, resulting in segregated, or separate, facilities for Black people that were inferior to what was available to white people. During the Jim Crow era, African Americans had to ride in separate train cars, seek treatment at separate hospitals, and attend separate schools from whites. Black people were forced to use segregated water fountains and ride at the back of buses, documented in plenty of photos of the time. In courts, separate Bibles were used for Black and white witnesses. And, particularly in Southern states, Black people were prevented from exercising their legal right to vote, with the creation of tests and poll taxes. (As mentioned in this book's introduction, new legislative moves in 2021 in states like Georgia, Florida, and Texas to limit how people vote harken back to this original period of Jim Crow.) All this was to maintain the divisions in US society that first came into effect during slavery.

Yet many people and organizations confronted these injustices. The National Association for the Advancement of Colored People, or NAACP, was founded in 1909 by scholar W. E. B. Du Bois and journalists Ida B. Wells and Mary White Ovington, among others, in response to an attack against the Black community in Springfield, Illinois. The group's goal was to end Jim Crow policies and push for African Americans to have equal rights in the truest sense. The NAACP was the most well-known civil rights organization of the twentieth century, though there would be many other organizations created over the years that worked toward similar goals in different parts of the country. These groups included the National Urban League, the Congress of Racial Equality, the Student Nonviolent Coordinating Committee, and the Black Panther Party, all groups that were predecessors to the Black Lives Matter movement of the twenty-first century.

V. An Ongoing Terror

By the early 1900s, Black people in the South were experiencing racial terrorism. A large white supremacist organization called the Ku Klux Klan (KKK), first formed in 1865 in Tennessee and later relaunched in 1915 in Georgia, became known for their acts of murder and intimidation of African Americans. This second rise of the KKK was spurred by the film *The Birth of a Nation*, to be discussed in Chapter 5, which looks at film and TV depictions of Black people.

Violence was an ongoing reality for Black people in the South. Since 1877, thousands of African Americans have been murdered by whites in a form of racial violence called lynching. Black people were killed in gruesome ways, including being hanged, burned to death, or shot. Some white Southerners would even have large picnics at lynchings, taking photos with corpses to showcase what was done. These acts were so frequent that much of the early work of the NAACP focused on trying to end lynchings and increase public awareness of these crimes.

African Americans regularly endured trauma as they simply tried to live. "People weren't lynched just because they were accused of some violent crime; they were lynched because they were successful in business," civil rights attorney and author Bryan Stevenson told the radio program *On the Media*. "They were lynched because they insisted on being treated fairly. When they asked for better wages as sharecroppers, they would be lynched. When they asked for better conditions as coal miners, they would be lynched. When a Black man got too close to a white woman, he would be lynched. When a Black woman complained about her husband being lynched being unjust, she would be lynched. And this violence was intended to sustain racial hierarchy."

A famous example of lynching is the 1955 murder of Emmett Till. The Chicago native was only fourteen years old at the time of his death. While visiting Mississippi, Till was kidnapped by two white men, beaten, shot in the head, and thrown into the Tallahatchie River. Why did they do this?

A CLOSER LOOK: THE TULSA MASSACRE OF 1921

Despite the housing discrimination that affected where and how they lived, some Black people were still able to invest in their own neighborhoods. By the early 1900s, the Greenwood District of Tulsa, Oklahoma, had a thriving African American community, with banks, stores, schools, libraries, hotels, and places of leisure. Educator Booker T. Washington had called the area "Black Wall Street"—an indication of its prosperity. Yet on May 31, 1921, a white mob, full of resentment and granted military-like powers, rampaged through the neighborhood, killing as many as three hundred Black people and destroying more than 1,400 homes and businesses. Thirty-five blocks burned to the ground. This was a massive act of lynching, of Black people being murdered for daring to excel amid oppression.

By the end of the onslaught, around ten thousand African Americans were left homeless and traumatized. Former residents of Greenwood weren't allowed to rebuild due to city regulations and weren't compensated for the loss of property and wealth. The community never recovered and much of the massacre was covered up by white officials. Hundreds of Black people were killed by white mobs in similar acts of hate in other community attacks before Tulsa, including the Red Summer of 1919, as well as the 1923 Rosewood Massacre in Florida.

A white woman had accused Till of whistling and touching her. Till's mother, Mamie, chose to leave the casket open at her son's funeral so the world could witness the brutality of the men who had murdered him.

The pair accused of the crime were acquitted by an all-white jury. Years later, the Mississippi woman who made the accusations against Till admitted that no such thing had happened. Of course, Till should never have been attacked even if the accusations were true.

VI. The Great Migration

Black people were also subject to other forms of physical and emotional violence, including the use of racial slurs and insults in speech and media. The purpose of all this was to humiliate, to constantly remind people of the codes of the land. To escape this terror and the harsh rules of segregation while seeking out better work opportunities, around six million Black people moved from the South to the northern, midwestern, and western regions of America throughout much of the twentieth century. Many left in secret, knowing that their travels would be sabotaged by whites if they revealed their plans. This massive movement of people—the largest movement of people ever seen in the United States—is known as the Great Migration. Some of the most celebrated figures of our time, including athlete Jesse Owens, soul-pop-rock star Prince, attorney and First Lady Michelle Obama, and, as mentioned before, author Toni Morrison, pursued careers made possible by this migration.

"Every four days somewhere in the American South in the first four decades of the twentieth century, someone was lynched for some perceived breach of [the established] caste system," said Isabel Wilkerson to the *Ted Radio Hour.* "And so this was what they were fleeing. I often say that this migration was not about geography. It was about freedom and how far people are willing [to go] to achieve it. It was really a defection, you know, seeking of political asylum. They became, in some ways, like political refugees within their own country."

The National Memorial for Peace and Justice opened in

April 2018 in Montgomery, Alabama, to remember those who were murdered as a result of lynching.

A CLOSER LOOK: JIM CROW LAWS OUTSIDE THE SOUTH

Southern states are historically known for their blatant Jim Crow policies, with signs at shops that read "Whites Only." But northern, midwestern, and western states also had a long history of official and unofficial codes that discriminated against Black people. These codes may not have been called Jim Crow laws, but they were still meant to maintain caste. As writer James Baldwin once wrote in an *Esquire* article about African Americans leaving the South, "They do not escape jim crow [sic]: they merely encounter another, not-less-deadly variety." Predominantly white factories of the North discriminated against African American workers, barring entry to higher positions of work. The New York entertainment venue the Cotton Club would feature Black people in the primarily Black neighborhood of Harlem performing for a whites-only audience. And in the city of Las Vegas, most casinos had whites-only policies, with desegregation gradually occurring in the 1950s.

One of the biggest civil rights protests of the 1960s took place in New York City, an area often associated with forward-thinking values. In 1964, almost half a million mostly Black and Puerto Rican students protested segregation in their schools, which were underfinanced and overcrowded. Yet even with such protests, segregated schools continued to remain an issue. In fact, since 1988, US public schools have become more segregated, the result of what *New York Times* columnist Nicholas Kristof calls a "Jim Crow financing system."

VII. The End of Jim Crow?

Due to the steadfast efforts of individuals and civil rights organizations, Jim Crow laws started to be slowly taken apart in the 1940s. During this time, a series of Supreme Court rulings pushed back against policies that discriminated against Black citizens, culminating in *Brown v. Board of Education of Topeka*. The NAACP Legal Defense and Education Fund, led by attorney and future Supreme Court justice Thurgood Marshall, brought the 1954 case to the highest court of the land. The *Brown v. Board of Education* ruling declared that segregation in public schools was unconstitutional.

A CLOSER LOOK: *BROWN V. BOARD OF EDUCATION*

Scholar **Ibram X. Kendi**, the author of best-selling books like *Stamped: Racism, Antiracism, and You*, has pointed out that a major issue with *Brown v. Board of Education* is that it's an "assimilationist idea." The court's ruling didn't acknowledge that white children were also being negatively affected in their development because of segregation. As a result, there was a push to integrate Black children into mostly white schools, motivated by the presumption that going to white schools would lead to a superior experience. An alternative, less assimilationist idea would have involved providing more resources to Black schools.

The ruling paved the way to end other forms of segregation and discrimination nationwide. But, as we also saw after the Reconstruction era, Southern legislatures reacted by passing dozens of new Jim Crow laws after the *Brown* ruling.

Nonetheless, civil rights efforts continued to grow in power. Over several years, well into the 1960s, waves of people across the South and other parts of America participated in massive, highly organized, intergenerational protest movements. These movements consisted of demonstrations, marches, and sit-ins broadcasted on TV and radio throughout the world. Important figures from this time included world-famous spiritual leaders Dr. Martin Luther King Jr. and Coretta Scott King, gay organizer Bayard Rustin, future congressman John Lewis, voting rights activist Fannie Lou Hamer, educator and author Angela Davis, and many others.

President Lyndon B. Johnson eventually signed the Civil Rights Act of 1964 despite a two-month filibuster led by Southern senators who tried to stop the bill. This legally ended segregation in the public sphere and officially barred different types of discrimination. Yet, as Dr. Hassett-Walker pointed out earlier, just because a law was passed didn't mean that citizens magically had a change in attitude. The same ideas of division seen at the country's founding hundreds of years ago persisted. America's layered legacy—a reliance on laws that allowed millions of people to be treated in deplorable ways by others—would continue to shape society for generations to come, even after the Civil Rights Act.

LET'S TALK ABOUT IT

* How does our presentation of what happened after the Civil War connect with what you've learned previously about this era? What were you most surprised to read? Why?

* Name two or three examples of Jim Crow policies, whether in the South or outside of the South.

* Why do you think so many white communities worked so hard to enforce Jim Crow laws? Why couldn't they embrace equality? What would have been the benefit of oppressing Black citizens?

* Think about what we've discussed about Jim Crow and caste. How does the case of Emmett Till serve as an example of these ideas?

* The chapter ended with a focus on the concept of American legacy. Can you think of any social circumstances currently seen in the US that might be the result of what we've discussed?

CHAPTER 3
PRISONS AND POLICING IN AMERICA

On a hot mid-June day in 2020, jazz pianist Jon Batiste sat in front of the sports and entertainment venue the Barclays Center in Brooklyn, New York. He was surrounded by an attentive crowd as he started his concert, his piano covered in bright rainbow stripes and silhouettes of human faces.

The city was grappling with the COVID-19 pandemic, so Batiste wore a mask for this special moment of protest and activism; a recognition of national, collective grief. He played the US national anthem, "The Star-Spangled Banner." He was aware of the history of discrimination in America, of the true legacy of the Founders who'd enslaved others. His performance of the anthem needed to reflect what he knew, and so he reinterpreted the tune in the tradition of other Black artists like Jimi Hendrix and Whitney Houston.

About a week earlier, honoring his New Orleans roots, Batiste had led a march appropriately called "We Are" through lower Manhattan. The march was attended by thousands, with fellow musicians playing tunes like the Black national anthem "Lift Every Voice and Sing" as well as "Respect" and "Empire State of Mind." And a week after the Barclays concert, Batiste performed in front of the Brooklyn Public Library to honor the African American holiday Juneteenth.

The New York protests were part of countless demonstrations that filled the streets of America during the summer of 2020 in reaction to the event that shook the world. On May 25, George Floyd, an unarmed African American citizen, was murdered by a white policeman who kept his knee on Floyd's neck for more than nine minutes, despite Floyd's urgent pleas for life, despite bystanders begging the officer to stop. The killing was caught on video during a time when millions of people were forced to stay home during a pandemic and stare at calmly rendered, senseless violence. The act was emblematic of a larger history.

A CLOSER LOOK: GEORGE FLOYD

On May 25, 2020, a forty-six-year-old African American man named **George Floyd** was killed by white police officer Derek Chauvin. Police were called in by a store clerk to confront Floyd, who was accused of using a counterfeit twenty-dollar bill. The ordeal was captured on a cellphone video taken by seventeen-year-old Darnella Frazier.

Waves of global protests sprung forth, highlighting issues of police brutality and social inequality that Black people have long faced. Across America, twenty-six million people of all backgrounds participated in more than seven thousand antiracist demonstrations, the largest mass protest in the country's history. The Black Lives Matter movement took center stage with its call for real change. Protestors presented a long list of Black people who had been killed by police, including Oscar Grant, Michael Brown, Tamir Rice, Philando Castile, and Breonna Taylor. The Floyd murder also pushed different industries to deal more directly with racial justice.

After a televised trial, Chauvin was convicted on April 20, 2021, of unintentional second-degree murder, third-degree murder, and second-degree manslaughter. The memory of George Floyd continues to be honored throughout the world.

In our previous chapter, we detailed how Black people were policed after the end of slavery, and how in certain parts of the South they could be arrested for the simple act of standing around in their neighborhood. And, as stated in the Thirteenth Amendment, once arrested, their newly won freedom could be taken away. These standards of policing have had far-reaching implications for Black people's relationship with a criminal justice system that, like the founding of the country, has been shaped by bias.

II. The Policing of Black America

Our ideas around policing are often informed by the cop TV shows and films we see on our screens, but the history of the profession is more complicated and nuanced. The very concept of being on patrol in the colonies was sometimes connected to enforcing slavery. Some of the first policing patrols that appeared in the southern colonies in the early 1700s were meant to control enslaved African Americans. These patrols wanted to ensure that there were no rebellions against slaveholders. White men were required to serve in these groups, which were maintained all the way to the end of the Civil War in 1865. Laws were also enacted in the South that prevented African Americans, whether free or enslaved, from possessing firearms like their white counterparts due to fear of an uprising. Those found with firearms could be whipped without a trial.

During this time period, the South hadn't established a police system in the same way that Northern states had. The first big municipal police department that resembles the systems we know today was created in 1838 in Boston, Massachusetts. By the end of the 1800s, this type of police force was the norm for major American cities. Still, these departments were influenced by powerful politicians who had their own agendas. While dealing with standard issues around crime and public safety, police could also be deployed against labor unions and newer waves of European immigrants.

Some Black people who moved north during the Great Migration found themselves policed unfairly after seeking refuge from the terrors of the South. Activists like Anna Thompson of the National Urban League and W. E. B. Du Bois would detail the disproportionate arrests and harassment of African Americans over the years. By the time of the massive March on Washington in 1963, many protestors were calling for an end to police brutality in Black communities among their list of demands.

By the late 1960s, protests and rebellions were taking place in various urban neighborhoods throughout the country in reaction to persistently terrible living conditions and traumatic events like the assassination of Martin Luther King Jr. These acts of unrest, some of which were sparked by police actions, were then used to justify more intense policing. President Johnson's Omnibus Crime Control and Safe Streets Act, which he signed into law in 1968, took funding away from social programs—considered by researchers to be an important element in preventing crime—and gave them to the police. After Richard Nixon became president in 1969, this concept of a war on crime was escalated even further. Politicians created language around maintaining "law and order." This meant that police forces could now crack down on everything from civil rights protests to legitimate crimes like muggings and assault.

The "extreme violence of the 1960s" has had long-term consequences for the country, according to Elizabeth Hinton, author of *America on Fire: The Untold History of Police Violence and Black Rebellion Since the 1960s*. "The enduring aftershocks have been felt more regularly, and more acutely, by Black people in American cities," she wrote in a special essay for the *New York Times*. "Alongside the rollout of civil rights legislation and the programs of the war on poverty, Black Americans faced new policing practices that emerged under the banner of the so-called war on crime: the routine stop and frisks that attacked people's dignity, the breaking up of community gatherings, the presence of armed, uniformed officers in the hallways of otherwise underresourced public schools, to give just a few examples."

Hinton sees the police and certain communities as caught in cycles of violence. Poorer Black communities are policed in ways that differ significantly from white communities with more resources. (In the next chapter, we'll look at how separate Black and white neighborhoods were created throughout the country.) Over the decades, racial profiling has been well documented in various parts of America, with officers utilizing stop and frisk tactics against people of color in a way that they would never do with white citizens. Attorney and journalist Josie Duffy Rice has referred to this as a "Jim Crow system of public safety."

During the late '60s, some government officials argued

WHAT DOES *THAT* MEAN?

Using ***stop and frisk*** policies, police officers can literally stop someone who they view as suspicious, and frisk, or pat, them down to see if they're carrying weapons or drugs. New York City became infamous for the use of stop and frisk in the early 2000s. The New York Civil Liberties Union found that there have been more than five million cases of stop and frisk in the city since 2002. The numbers peaked in 2011 under Mayor Michael Bloomberg's tenure and have gone down dramatically under the Bill de Blasio administration. Almost 90 percent of those being stopped by police were innocent of anything illegal, with young Black and Latinx males far more targeted than other groups due to racial profiling.

Racial profiling is seen most notably with traffic stops. According to a 2015 report from the Department of Justice, around half of the fifty million people who encountered police did so as the result of being pulled over, with Black people disproportionately stopped.

that an increased police presence in neighborhoods with fewer resources was the best way to halt crimes in these communities. These decisions were made without looking at what actually caused crimes in these areas. Considering the causes of crime would be considered a holistic approach, looking at how entire systems work, as opposed to looking only at individual actions. While working in law enforcement can indeed be dangerous, the power given to police in urban areas has also resulted in a long list of unarmed people who, like George Floyd, were taken out in simple acts of living: Amadou Diallo, a West African immigrant in the Bronx who was killed in a hail of bullets from officers as he tried to take out his wallet; Eric Garner, a Staten Island dad who died in an officer's illegal chokehold after being stopped for selling untaxed cigarettes; Tamir Rice, a twelve-year-old in Cleveland with a toy gun who was shot within two seconds of police arriving on the scene; and Breonna Taylor, a Louisville emergency room technician who was killed by shots from police when they entered her apartment over suspicion of drug possession by an ex-boyfriend.

III. Calls for Change

For decades, researchers have asserted that the way to deal with inner-city crime is *not* to give police unchecked power but instead to provide resources for neighborhood residents.

The Kerner Commission was formed by President Johnson after the wave of urban riots of 1967, when dozens of people were killed in the cities of Detroit and Newark alone. While citing the atmosphere of fear felt by inner-city residents and police alike, the commission called for an end to over-policing for petty crimes that did not endanger lives or property. The commission also recommended that the government provide Black neighborhoods with better economic and social resources so that residents could have the same opportunities as other Americans. Black people needed much better access to adequate housing, jobs, lines of credit, and governmental participation. To put it simply, discrimination needed to end for urban violence to end.

The commission's report ultimately asserted, "Our nation is moving toward two societies, one black, one white—separate and unequal." Keep in mind this conclusion was made after the rulings of *Brown v. Board of Education* and the 1964 Civil Rights Act, which were technically supposed to end segregation. (Remember our mention of these items in Chapter 2?) Many people championed the Kerner report's findings—it was published as a book and became a best seller—but both Presidents Johnson and Nixon chose not to follow the commission's advice.

More than fifty years after the Kerner report, researchers and scholars today still say that urban violence can be greatly reduced by providing resources to communities. And they remind us that the ideas around reducing crime deserve to be looked at holistically, with some activists calling for the defunding of the police as others demand police reform. Even with their conflicting ideas, these organizations agree on the need for change. Spurred on by the Black Lives Matter movement and the protests of 2020, city governments have started to look at how communities can create their own forms of policing. Some areas have begun to rely on special dispatchers to handle emergency calls related to mental illness or addiction, as seen with the CAHOOTS program in Eugene, Oregon. And in Berkeley, California, a special department of transportation has been created for traffic violations, removing armed police from encounters meant to be nonviolent.

IN THE MEDIA: IS REALITY TV REAL? THE CASE OF *COPS*

After the murder of **George Floyd**, the long-running

reality TV show *Cops* was canceled in 2020 in America after thirty-two seasons. This show was controversial for its depiction of patrols and arrests, but these depictions often didn't match what we know about real-world policing, even though the show was marketed as reality TV. Black and brown people on *Cops* were way more likely to be associated with violent crime than they were in real life, according to statistics. And violent crimes were given way more screen time on the show, compared to their occurrence in the real world.

The group **Color of Change** had successfully campaigned against Fox to have the show removed from its network in 2013. The group then pushed the Paramount network to cancel the show after the killing of George Floyd. A similar reality show, *Live PD*, was canceled, too. Going beyond these two programs, both reality and fictitious cop shows have been accused of presenting ideas about policing that aren't true. For instance, did you know that most cases are plea bargained, never reaching court?

IV. America's Unique Position

Systems of mass incarceration go hand in hand with the systems of policing we just touched on. The criminal justice system in America has long been seen by many as harsh and unfair to everyone, regardless of race, because of the country's super-high rate of imprisonment.

WHAT'S THAT WORD?

Incarceration (say: in-kar-suh-RAY-shun) is the act of putting people in jail or prison. ***Mass incarceration*** is a phrase used to describe the high rates of imprisonment we see in the United States, with the term *mass* referring to large numbers of people. The 1970s was when the modern mass incarceration era in America began. Yet there has been some objection to this term. Though meant to be helpful, some say the phrase erases the trauma experienced by someone who might be unfairly sent to jail or prison.

Almost one out of every one hundred people in America is in prison or jail. This makes the United States the country with the highest rate of incarceration in the world by far, even compared to nations considered to have oppressive governments. In fact, even states with "low" incarceration, like Massachusetts and Vermont, have higher rates than almost all other countries. As of 2019, though America has less than 5 percent of the world's general population, the country has more than 20 percent of the world's imprisoned population.

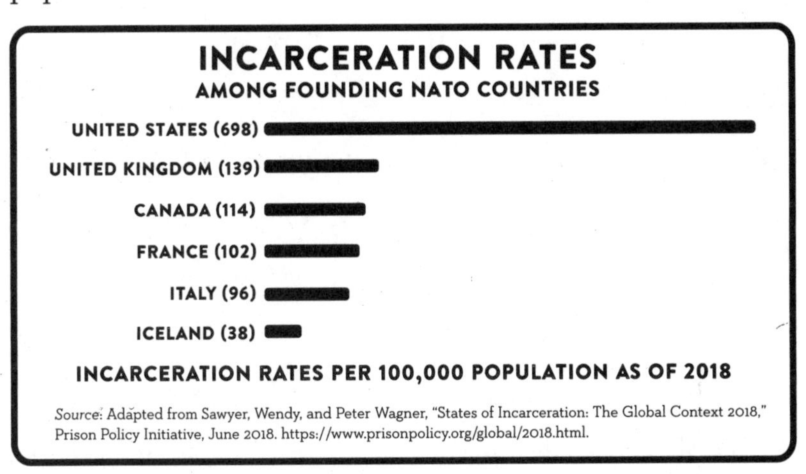

Source: Adapted from Sawyer, Wendy, and Peter Wagner, "States of Incarceration: The Global Context 2018," Prison Policy Initiative, June 2018. https://www.prisonpolicy.org/global/2018.html.

Many scholars have declared that, for Black people, the prison system is a continuation of the Jim Crow laws that came into effect after the Thirteenth Amendment. Sociologist and writer Dr. Reuben Jonathan Miller believes in this historical thread. In his book, *Halfway Home: Race, Punishment, and the Afterlife of Mass Incarceration*, he asserts: "To live through mass incarceration is to take part in a lineage of control that can be traced from the slave ships, through the Jim Crow South, to the ghettos of the North, and to the many millions of almost-always-filled bunk beds in jails and prison cells that make the United States the world's leading jailer."

America's current prison system was modeled after Eastern State Penitentiary, which opened in 1829 in Philadelphia, Pennsylvania. Founded by Quakers, the system was supposed to encourage prisoners to reflect on their actions and express regret over the crimes they committed. Prisoners were completely isolated from one another in a manner that we now call solitary confinement. The forced isolation of the prisoners caused emotional distress, so this practice was done away with at the facility as a general rule. Nonetheless, Eastern served as a model for the design of future prisons. Many of the debates around what prisons should look like and how people should be treated inside their walls stem from Eastern.

Decades later, by the time of Black codes and Jim Crow laws, prisons in the South had taken the form of farms and labor camps. As stated in Chapter 2, many African Americans could easily be arrested for things that we wouldn't consider a crime today and taken to these farms or camps. The conditions there were terrible, in some cases worse than what people had lived through while enslaved.

"Sometimes there were visitors who would show up at one of these camps where almost no one ever came, and they would find dozens of Black men laboring in the fields or in the forest with no clothing on at all in an emaciated state—people with missing arms and legs," said Pulitzer Prize–winning historian Douglas Blackmon, in an interview with the radio show *Throughline*. "And there was a phrase at the time that if someone working in these camps died, that this was no big deal because, quote-unquote, 'one dies, get another.'"

By the twentieth century, the chain gang system was introduced into state prison systems in the South. In this type of imprisonment, men would be literally chained together as they built roads or dug ditches. And those subjected to the harsh chain gang and convict leasing systems were predominantly Black. Very few white prisoners were forced to labor in such a way.

Black people being imprisoned and made to work in this way connects to what we discussed earlier about the time immediately after the Civil War, about the persistence of caste and systemic racism. According to attorney and author Bryan Stevenson, "The 13th Amendment is credited with ending slavery, but it stopped short of that: It made an exception for those convicted of crimes. After emancipation, black people, once seen as less than fully human 'slaves,' were seen as less than fully human 'criminals.' . . . Laws governing slavery were replaced with Black Codes governing free black people—making the criminal-justice system central to new strategies of racial control."

Authorities had established a different type of prison system in the North that was nonetheless also hostile to Black citizens. After a rise in violent crime in the 1920s, the prison population grew significantly, fueled by factors like public fear and mandatory sentencing laws. Many African Americans made their way north during the Great Migration, but the prison population in the states where they settled became even more disproportionately Black because of over-policing.

To explain these higher rates of imprisonment, some social scientists put forth the idea that Black people were inferior and prone to criminal behavior. Frederick Hoffman, a German statistician who moved to the United States in 1886, presented theories that claimed Black people were biologically more criminal. Such ideas helped to rationalize why Black people occupied the lowest caste in America. They also let white institutions off the hook when it came to addressing inequality.

V. America's Incarceration Boom

As a result of the governmental emphasis on law and order that became popular during the late 1960s, America's prison population exploded in a way that had never been seen before. More people in the country were sent to prison between 1965 and 1982—a less than twenty-year period—than between 1865 and 1964!

This dramatic surge was part of a larger incarceration boom that would go on for decades. The prison population in America numbered less than 360,000 in 1970, but by the new millennium had increased to more than two million people. In 1980, around 40,900 people were imprisoned for drug offenses; by 2019, that number had grown to 430,926 people. On top of all of this, people started serving longer times in prison if they were convicted of a federal drug offense.

According to the Prison Policy Initiative, "the U.S. has been engaged in a globally unprecedented experiment to make every part of its criminal justice system more expansive and more punitive. As a result, incarceration has become the nation's default response to crime, with, for example, 70 percent of convictions resulting in confinement—far more than other developed nations with comparable crime rates."

Just as was the case with the convict leasing and chain gangs, Black communities have suffered the most under the criminal justice system, often becoming the targets of police in neighborhoods they're forced to live in because of Jim Crow–type policies. The war on crime that marked the late 1960s was followed by a war on drugs, another initiative spearheaded by the Nixon presidential administration, and then the Ronald Reagan administration of the 1980s.

A CLOSER LOOK: THE ROLE OF ART IN CRIMINAL JUSTICE

Katie Yamasaki is an acclaimed muralist, painter, and children's book author based in Brooklyn, New York. She has also worked with art programs within the criminal justice system on an international level. One program, Transformation from the Inside Out, worked with imprisoned women as well as their children. Yamasaki sees her job as helping people who've been incarcerated or impacted by incarceration to tell their story through their own words and images, defying perceptions of the larger world. She's guided the creation of a variety of community installations and murals, including *Heavy Blanket* in Philadelphia, Pennsylvania, and *If Walls Could*

Talk in Harlem, New York.

"A lot of this has to do with decriminalizing trauma," Yamasaki said in an exclusive interview for True History. "One thing that I've really observed most present with everybody that I've worked with is, at the base of whatever has happened is something very traumatic. Some people are just born into trauma." Yamasaki is speaking of people who are born into physical abuse, sexual abuse, poverty, and high levels of stress, who are criminalized for being born into this system as opposed to being provided with resources—a belief that echoes the findings of the Kerner Commission. "A lot of the goals for me with this work is to kind of humanize the story so that people from all walks of life can identify with people who are incarcerated, not as incarcerated people but as people who have gone through something really terrible and are being punished, usually pretty unfairly."

Yamasaki was inspired to get into this work by the experiences of her own ancestors. Some of Yamasaki's Japanese family members were subjected to mass incarceration as well. During World War II, the US government forced around 120,000 people of Japanese descent to live in large camps based on fears that they might be spies. There was no evidence to support this assumption and most of those imprisoned were American. She has written and illustrated a book about her Uncle Jimmy, who as a child was forced to live in one of these camps.

VI. The Rockefeller Drug Laws

In the mid-1970s, New York governor Nelson Rockefeller put forth what would come to be known as the Rockefeller Drug Laws. These laws were noted for their harshness and were supposedly meant to deter drug-related misconduct in a city grappling with high rates of crime, financial issues, and unrelenting grime. Those caught possessing or selling even small amounts of drugs received a mandatory sentence of fifteen years to life in prison. Other states, along with the federal government, adopted similar measures.

But over time, observers realized that the overwhelming majority of people being arrested and imprisoned for these offenses were Black and Latinx. This was the case even though studies showed that white people used drugs at similar rates. In fact, according to one New York governmental study, the majority of drug users in the state were white. The Rockefeller Drug Laws did not encourage police to do the legwork of tracking down offenders who were actually dangerous to others. Instead, many people of color who had committed no acts of violence were policed where they lived, treated like criminals, and thrown into jail.

The disproportionate arrests and imprisonment of people of color have continued for decades as part of the incarceration boom that saw the construction of many new prisons. This phenomenon has been referred to as the prison industrial complex. By the end of 2018, Black people were imprisoned at more than *five* times the rate of white people, and twice the rate of Latinx people. While Black people make up around 14 percent of America's population, as of 2018, they represented 33 percent of the prison population. African American men are particularly jailed and imprisoned at much higher rates than any other ethnic/racial group and the country, and people of color make up 67 percent of the prison population as compared to 37 percent of the general population. And while the rate of incarceration for juvenile offenders has been declining since 1999, youth of color make up two-thirds of juvenile offenders held in custody. They are also more likely to receive tougher sentences than their white counterparts for the same crime. Those who've suffered the most under

America's original system of bondage also suffered the most under the country's criminal justice system centuries later.

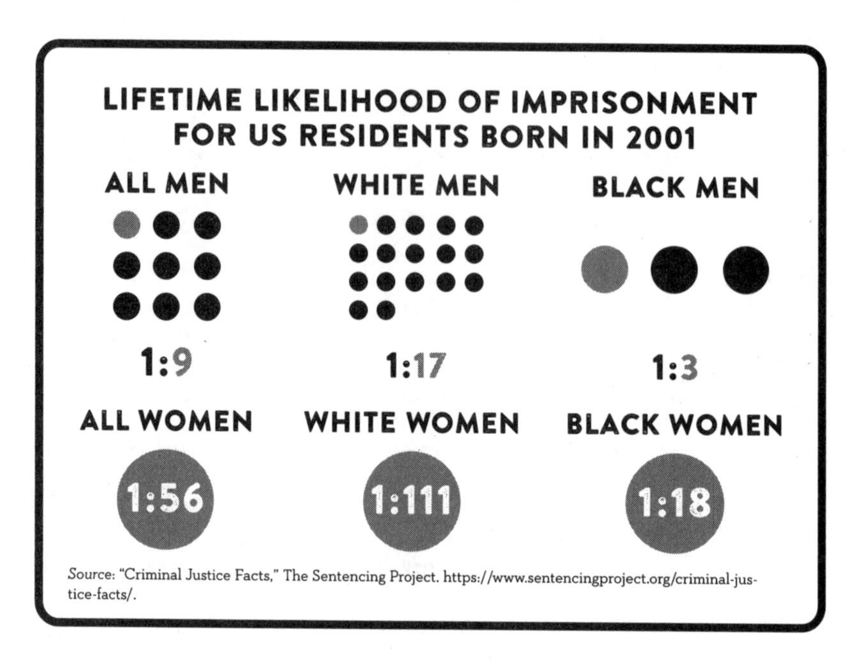

Source: "Criminal Justice Facts," The Sentencing Project. https://www.sentencingproject.org/criminal-justice-facts/.

"Generally younger people think that the court system and the criminal justice system are like what they see on TV. It's like perfect. Bad people get in trouble and they go to jail," said Roland R. Acevedo in an exclusive interview with True History. Acevedo is an attorney whose practice has dealt with different elements of the law, including social justice issues. "They have no idea that certain groups are targeted," he continued, "and I guess there are many reasons why people are targeted. It's an extension of Jim Crow." He cited the laws of New York City, where police are given more leeway to practice stop and frisk tactics in what are considered rougher neighborhoods. "The criminal justice system, as I often tell people, is just an extension of all the other systems you see in depressed neighborhoods."

In addition to calling for more nuanced understandings of who gets imprisoned, while acknowledging the need for some form of law enforcement, Acevedo also firmly believes in the power of access to education. In his eyes, it's the number one item that could cause a massive shift in incarceration as we know it. "Education is this wonderful equalizer," said Acevedo, who sees value in a range of professions. "If you look at the stats, people who get college educations while in prison, their recidivism rate is microscopic."

Recidivism is the term used to reference people returning to jail after they've previously been arrested. Echoing Acevedo's claim, according to a study from the Bureau of Justice looking at thirty states, the recidivism rate for people with a bachelor's degree was less than 6 percent, far lower than the general recidivism rate, which can be as high as 75 percent. And absolutely no one who'd earned a master's degree returned to prison.

A CLOSER LOOK: THE EXONERATED FIVE

In 1989, during a time when New York City was notorious for its high crime rates, a twenty-eight-year-old white woman named Trisha Meili was found horribly beaten and raped in Central Park. Five teenagers of color—**Raymond Santana**, **Antron McCray**, **Kevin Richardson**, **Yusef Salaam**, and **Korey Wise**, ages fourteen to sixteen—were in the park at the time of the crime. They were arrested and interrogated by police. Due to the inhumane conditions of the interrogation, the five confessed to a crime they didn't commit. They later retracted their confessions but were still convicted at trial. The coverage of the case was sensational, and the language used to describe the accused boys highlighted how Black males were historically depicted in the media. They were called "animals" and "savages" by professional news outlets.

In 2002, Matias Reyes, a convicted murderer and serial rapist, admitted to the crime against Meili. DNA testing verified his confession. By the end of that year, the convictions against the five were dismissed. Still, they had all served time for a crime they didn't commit. Several of the five now work as advocates for criminal justice reform. The Exonerated Five's story has been dramatized in the Ava DuVernay TV miniseries *When They See Us* and Yusef Salaam has written about his experience in the 2021 memoir *Better, Not Bitter.*

VII. A Complex Issue

Even while being aware of racial biases, it's important to note that the issues of mass incarceration and policing in America are very complex. Some journalists and politicians have paid a lot of attention to the cases of nonviolent drug offenders in federal prisons, particularly those arrested as a result of the harsh drug laws mentioned earlier. Some have even implied that eliminating imprisonment for these types of crimes would pretty much end mass incarceration. But most people are held at state and local facilities, not federal prisons. And most of those held at state and local facilities were imprisoned for offenses that have nothing to do with drugs.

The more recent increases in mass incarceration were also fueled by a boom in the number of prosecutors pursuing cases starting in the mid-1990s, even though by this time, the rate of crime had begun to fall. This means that certain government attorneys are choosing to bring charges against offenses that government attorneys in previous decades would not have pursued.

On top of all of this, deadly weapons are very much in the mix when it comes to conflicts in the United States. Police forces use military-style equipment to do their job while American civilians have more guns than the populace of any other nation on the planet. These webs of violence particularly hurt the most vulnerable and reinforce the idea that imprisonment is the primary solution for crime in America.

"You know, why did we make a world in which 49 percent of Black men will be arrested before they're twenty-three and 38 percent of white men will be arrested before they turn twenty-three?" Miller said to journalist Terry Gross in 2021. "I want us to think about all these traps that we've created, we've produced, and I want us to unmake them. That's my hope."

LET'S TALK ABOUT IT

* How much do you remember about the protests of 2020? We profiled Jon Batiste's piano playing earlier. Are there other forms of art and creativity that you associate with this time period or with the protests?
* How have you been impacted by the case of George Floyd? What discussions have you had about his case? What connections do you see between his case and that of the Exonerated Five?
* Why do you think presidents and policy makers have ignored the recommendations of the Kerner Commission? Do you agree with the commission's findings? Why or why not?
* Why do you think crime is so closely associated with neighborhoods that have less resources? Please explain in detail.
* Keeping in mind our short discussion of *Cops*, how are criminals and police portrayed on the TV shows or movies that you've watched? Which screen portrayals were the most interesting or compelling to you? Why?

CHAPTER 4
THE IMPACT OF HOUSING DISCRIMINATION

In spring 2021, famed journalist Linda Villarosa detailed her return to her old Chicago, Illinois, neighborhood for *New York Times Magazine*. Like author Toni Morrison, Villarosa's ancestors were part of the Great Migration from the South and had settled in the North during the 1920s. During Villarosa's trip with her mother to her former neighborhood, she was surprised to see how much of the area had vacant lots and how the house where she grew up seemed to be abandoned.

When she was growing up in Chicago, her parents were on the verge of moving the family to a nearby white suburb.

But a police officer there told her father that he couldn't guarantee the family's safety. They eventually relocated to the city of Lakewood in Colorado, only to have children in the neighborhood write a racial insult on their garage before their arrival. Villarosa's father was prepared to leave right away, but her parents decided to stay after neighbors tried to make amends. Her story captures much of the journey that African Americans have taken to try to find places to live where they could feel safe and thrive. Decisions about where to live in the United States are generally more complex and require more consideration for Black families than white families.

Though the South has been traditionally associated with rigid Jim Crow, other areas of the United States have instituted policies that were very discriminatory as well, which we briefly discussed in Chapter 2. These polices have had a huge impact on Black citizens for generations, especially when it comes to where people live.

"If you sought to advantage one group of Americans and disadvantage another, you could scarcely choose a more graceful method than housing discrimination," wrote journalist Ta-Nehisi Coates in an article for *The Atlantic* that looked at the question of reparations for African Americans.

Coates asserted that housing discrimination is a surefire way to maintain inequality. "Housing determines access to transportation, green spaces, decent schools, decent food, decent jobs, and decent services. Housing affects your chances of being robbed and shot as well as your chances of being stopped and frisked."

Coates's statements are born out of the history of housing access for African Americans. By the early 1900s, racial zoning was an acceptable practice. "City government could come up with racially designated blocks within a community and say, 'White people live here, Black people live there,'" professor and author Keeanga-Yamahtta Taylor told the radio program *All Things Considered*. "But a 1917 Supreme Court decision said that that was a clear violation of the Fourteenth Amendment." (Do you remember our mention of the Fourteenth Amendment? It gave certain rights of citizenship to African Americans, with an emphasis on property rights, too.)

As a result of the Supreme Court decision, real estate agents instead started to rely on racially restrictive covenants, or agreements. They placed a rider, or what's also known as a special clause, into a property's deed, declaring that homes could only be sold in the future to other whites. And sometimes these sales could only go to certain *types* of white people, excluding, for instance, immigrants from southern or eastern Europe.

A CLOSER LOOK: LANGUAGE FROM A CONTRACT

Racially restrictive covenants in the United States are well documented. Language taken from property deeds in West Hartford, Connecticut, during the 1940s stated that, "No persons of any race except the white race shall use or occupy any building on any lot except that this covenant shall not prevent occupancy by domestic servants of a different race employed by an owner or tenant." This means that only white people were allowed to own and live in a particular home except for the servants they employed, who could be non-white.

These restrictive covenants were done away with by the Supreme Court in 1948 with the case of *Shelley v. Kraemer.* The ruling again cited the Fourteenth Amendment as a reason for racial covenants being considered unlawful.

IN THE MEDIA: *A RAISIN IN THE SUN*

Lorraine Hansberry's *A Raisin in the Sun* opened on March 11, 1959, at the Ethel Barrymore Theatre in New York City. Hansberry, a trailblazer, was the first African American woman to write a Broadway play. The drama follows the Youngers, a 1950s Chicago South Side family that has received insurance money after the patriarch's death. The matriarch of the family puts a down payment on a home in Clybourne Park, a white neighborhood. A representative from a special association later comes to the Younger household to pay off the family to prevent them from moving into Clybourne. The representative wants to stop the area from becoming racially mixed.

Hansberry's childhood inspired the theatrical drama. Her family had moved into a white Chicago neighborhood and dealt with racist, violent neighbors. A brick was thrown into their home. Hansberry was physically bullied walking to school. Neighbors sued to force the family to leave based on restrictive housing covenants. Her father, a successful real estate agent, pushed back legally; he took his case all the way to the Supreme Court with the backing of the NAACP and won. In a later case, the court would eventually declare housing covenants unconstitutional.

Giving a textured snapshot of the challenges faced by African Americans, *A Raisin in the Sun* has become one of the most esteemed theatrical works ever produced.

II. The True Cost of Redlining

Other governmental actions in the twentieth century impacted how and where Black people lived, creating neighborhoods that have often been over-policed. After the Great Depression, the Federal Housing Administration (FHA) was founded by Congress in 1934. The organization helped to insure home loans made by banks. The FHA was also responsible for allowing people to make much lower down payments when buying their homes. But, in another example of systemic racism, Black people were not treated equally under FHA programs. The organization created maps of green, blue, and yellow, marking certain neighborhoods with certain colors. These colors acted as a grading system, with green areas seen as the most desirable and worthy of receiving FHA insurance. Red areas were considered the least desirable, and thus the term redlining was born. These redlined neighborhoods had old, worn-out buildings. The red grade also indicated the types of people moving into these neighborhoods, including Black people and immigrants. The federal government, through the FHA, chose not to invest money in these neighborhoods. Following the government's lead, private businesses also chose not to invest in redlined areas. This lack of investment was a major issue because businesses generally help to provide stability, wealth, and a nicer standard of life for neighborhoods.

The FHA also gave white homeowners small loans so that they could make repairs to their property. African Americans in redlined neighborhoods were excluded from receiving these loans. This meant they didn't have money to repair their homes, which would then impact the value of the property on the real estate market. And so the myth was created that African Americans were and still are inherently associated with "bad" neighborhoods.

This type of housing segregation, even though not technically labeled Jim Crow, nonetheless contributed to people having a more difficult life. Certain neighborhoods became ghettos. This term is no longer used as frequently as it once was, though it was a common way to define poor, urban neighborhoods for much of the twentieth century.

WHAT'S THAT WORD?

The term ***ghetto*** was first used in Venice, Italy, in the 1500s, referring to the small area of the city where Jewish people were forced to live. Centuries later, the word was used for areas in Europe where Jewish communities were relocated by the Nazis during World War II, as well as US neighborhoods where African Americans lived because of housing restrictions. Immigrants or people with lower incomes in America have also lived in ghettos. According to scholar Daniel Schwartz, who wrote a book on the history of the word, the term *ghetto* is "often associated with overcrowding, poverty and racial and religious segregation. When most of us think of ghettos, we picture people confined in dilapidated conditions against their will."

Yet, even with this history, Schwartz has pointed out that the word, like other elements of language, has a good amount of fluidity. Some people might call someone "ghetto" as an insult. And the same people might use the word in joyous, humorous ways, meant to conjure pride about where someone is from. (The author of this book, a native New Yorker, is proudly ghetto at times with his pals.) Outpourings of culture have originated from places marked as ghettos, including the Harlem Renaissance and the Black Arts movement. And other items that came from urban areas, like the musical genres salsa, hip-hop, and house, have become huge around the globe.

Because they weren't given access to the same modes of support as their white counterparts, Black people were targeted by lenders looking to make money off an unfair situation. During the 1950s, many African Americans couldn't own their homes in a traditional sense with a standard mortgage. Instead, they had contract leases, also called contracts for deeds. In these schemes, African Americans would enter into an agreement with a real estate agent or special company to one day own the deed to their house after making payments for decades. If they missed a single payment on their home, they could be evicted. They would have to give up their house and lose all of the money they'd already paid. Linda Villarosa's grandparents, for instance, purchased their home via contract leasing. The terms of this type of loan are now considered to be unethical, a practice known as predatory lending.

Another real estate practice that defined the twentieth century was blockbusting, which was also referred to as "panic peddling." In this scheme, real estate agents would tell white homeowners that African Americans would be moving into their neighborhood, selling a house to a Black family to illustrate this or sometimes even hiring Black people to walk through the neighborhood as proof of what was about to happen. This would put the targeted homeowners into a "panic," as real estate agents would imply that Black people moving into the area meant that property values were going to quickly decrease. The homeowners would sell to a real estate agent, who would then turn around and sell the same home to Black people at a much higher price. This higher price was inflated, which means that the new selling price to Black buyers was far above the general value of homes at the time. Black buyers were willing to pay these higher prices because they were often unable to purchase homes in neighborhoods they desired through regular real estate agents like their white counterparts. Real estate agents who worked as blockbusters could make lots of money from these deals.

Yet as more Black people arrived, home values would not rise. This was because of the belief that the presence of African Americans in a neighborhood meant that the area was less desirable, and so the properties were worth less. This practice would also contribute to what was known as "white flight," where white families moved to the suburbs (residential areas outside of cities) so as not to live with Black people. White flight would also contribute to the financial inequities faced by African American neighborhoods as white suburban areas had a higher tax base. Paying more taxes meant that you would get more resources from the local government for the upkeep of your neighborhood, whereas poorer neighborhoods didn't get the same attention. White flight meant that private white businesses left neighborhoods as well, further diminishing the area's tax base.

Blockbusting occurred in a variety of US cities or towns, including Chicago, Illinois; Bloomfield, Connecticut; Baltimore, Maryland; and Compton, California. In the case of Compton, in 1950, less than 1 percent of the city's population was non-white; by 1960, 40 percent of the population was Black.

Blockbusting, along with redlining, was officially abolished by the Fair Housing Act. This act was meant to bar discrimination when it came to the sale and renting of housing. Still, the legacy of US housing discrimination remains. People still engage in prejudicial behavior when it comes to providing housing to others. Remember a previous point from the time of Reconstruction—just because a law has changed doesn't mean that people's attitudes change.

III. Less Opportunities to Build Wealth and Stability

The long-term effect of housing discrimination is that Black people have been unable to build wealth at the same rate as those born into privilege. African Americans have not had the same opportunities as white citizens to invest in home ownership, which has traditionally been the primary form of wealth building in America. Sure enough, the average net worth of a white family in the United States is ten times that of a Black family's, with more than a third of Black households having no wealth at all.

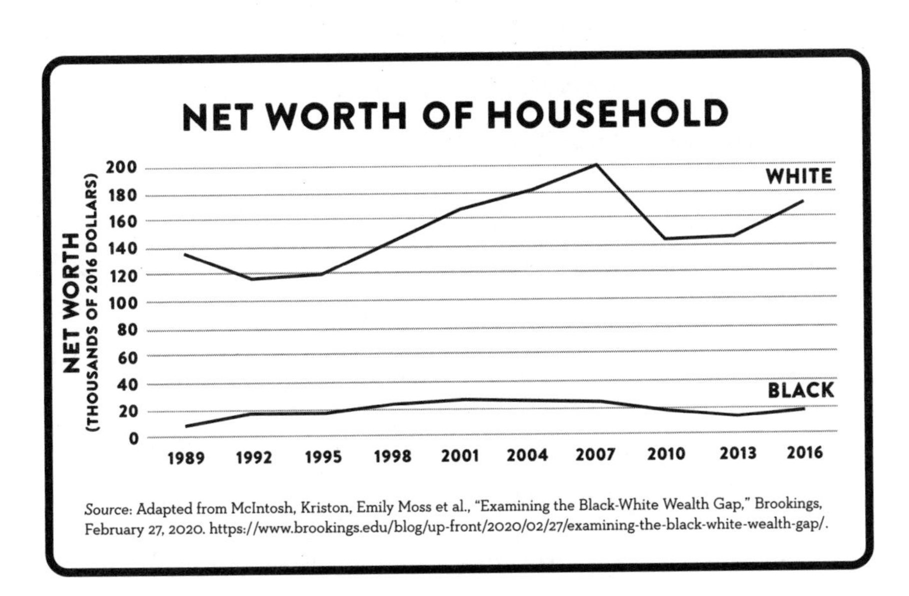

Source: Adapted from McIntosh, Kriston, Emily Moss et al., "Examining the Black-White Wealth Gap," Brookings, February 27, 2020. https://www.brookings.edu/blog/up-front/2020/02/27/examining-the-black-white-wealth-gap/.

This wealth discrepancy is largely a result of Black people having limited access to the housing market, along with discrepancies in areas like work income and educational opportunities. As of 2021, the gap between Black and white homeownership is larger than it was more than sixty years ago when Jim Crow–type laws were still in effect.

Even with these obstacles, Black people have still managed to create vibrant, economically stable communities, as seen with various areas in New York City; and Prince George's County, Maryland, a bit more to the south. Yet many predominantly Black areas suffer from a lack of resources that other neighborhoods take for granted, dealing with everything from overcrowded housing and limited public transportation to food deserts, which is when a neighborhood doesn't have supermarkets in the immediate area stocked with items that contribute to good health, like fresh fruits and veggies. (Some prefer the term "food apartheid" as opposed to "food deserts.") Areas with fewer resources have public schools that receive less funding from local governments, which affects what resources are available to students, which then affects what educational opportunities those students will have later in life.

The issue of how and where we live, along with the right to have fair access to quality housing and neighborhoods, is a fundamental part of the American experience.

LET'S TALK ABOUT IT

* Based on what we've discussed in previous chapters, why do you think African Americans have been targeted by housing discrimination practices? Are there any neighborhoods that you can think of not mentioned here that are the result of housing discrimination?
* How did practices like redlining contribute to the creation of what were called ghettos?

CHAPTER 5
HOW WE'RE SEEN ON THE SCREEN

On a late California afternoon in February 2019, actor Chadwick Boseman stepped onto the red carpet in front of the Dolby Theatre. He wore a long, black, sequined blazer that almost swept the ground. It was a noticeable departure from the standard tuxedos many men tend to wear to the Academy Awards ceremony, which was about to take place. It was an outfit some might say was fit for a king.

Cameras flashed. Videos were captured. Social media was abuzz. Boseman was a major part of a historical night. The movie in which he starred, the record-breaking *Black Panther*, was the first superhero movie to be nominated for an Academy Award (or Oscar, for short) in the category of Best Picture.

As many of you probably already know, Boseman played T'Challa, the thoughtful, revered monarch of the fictional country in Africa known as Wakanda. Other members of the cast, like Danai Gurira, Letitia Wright, and Michael B. Jordan, along with director, Ryan Coogler, arrived on the red carpet together. They basked in the energy of the night. Cast and director were the toast of the town not just because of the award recognition but because of the popularity of their film, the result of their diligence. *Black Panther* would bring in more than $700 million in North America, with around seventy-six million tickets sold, making it one of the top five highest-earning movies of all time in North America.

Yet, it once would have been unheard of for a film with a primarily Black cast to receive huge financial backing from Hollywood, much less be nominated for best film with actors front and center on the red carpet alongside everyone else. In fact, in 1940, the very first African American woman to receive an Oscar wasn't allowed to sit with other members of the cast of her film at the award ceremony because of the color of her skin, because of Jim Crow.

In previous chapters, we've looked at how Jim Crow concepts have shaped real-world history, including the Black codes, the criminal justice system, and housing discrimination. In this chapter, we're going to look at how we're depicted on stage and screen. Many portrayals of African Americans have been extremely distorted, contributing to negative stereotypes about Black people for decades. Some people have long believed that it's okay to treat Black communities in negative ways because of these stereotypes. Yet in recent times, we've seen an outpouring of projects that can be seen as correcting what has come before, with some creators aware of the past.

Detailing society's cultural output over the years is a humongous topic, and space prevents us from doing a deep dive. That said, we also know that this subject can be compelling and a lot of fun for readers to discuss because of how important media is in our lives.

II. The Tradition of Minstrelsy

As stated in Chapter 2, Jim Crow was a character created by a white entertainer in blackface, as part of the minstrel traditions of the 1800s.

WHAT'S THAT WORD?

Minstrels were white entertainers in blackface who would present extremely demeaning performances. They would distort how African Americans ate, moved, and talked, often with the purpose of making Black people appear to be ignorant, lazy, and objects of ridicule. The word *minstrel* was first used to describe entertainers from medieval times.

The tradition of blackface came from this time and later appeared in various forms throughout the twentieth century, including among white performers like singer-actors Al Jolson and Bing Crosby. But have you heard about when people were revealed to have put on blackface or brownface as seen more recently with Virginia governor Ralph Northam and Canadian prime minister Justin Trudeau before they held office? And did you know that in the United Kingdom, a program called *The Black and White Minstrel Show*, with white performers in blackface, ran for twenty years starting in 1958 on the government-financed TV channel the BBC?

Minstrelsy was very popular in the middle of the nineteenth century, with songs, dances, and comedy routines that made fun of African Americans. (Black people themselves were barred from appearing on major stages at this time.) Some minstrel shows would even focus on plantations—where enslaved people were beaten and tortured—as a source of humor. Major performance companies were part of this tradition that actually became popular in the North and parts of Europe. One company, Christy's Minstrels, appeared on Broadway for a decade. The distinct two-part format Christy's used for its shows came to be influential, and the Pittsburgh-born songwriter Stephen Foster, known for his song "Oh! Susanna," wrote minstrel songs for the company.

NOW LET'S TAKE A MOMENT . . .

Yes, this might be hard to believe. While the civil rights movement was in full swing in America during the 1950s and '60s, followed by the Black is Beautiful cultural movement of the '60s and '70s, England aired a TV show with a parade of singing, dancing white men in blackface. Some of the performers in *The Black and White Minstrel Show* would later state that they didn't realize just how offensive the show was, perhaps not having researched the history of minstrelsy. One performer said in an interview that R&B legend Diana Ross, upon seeing these men in makeup during a rehearsal at the London Palladium, refused to sing until they left the auditorium.

JOINT RESOLUTION TO ABOLISH SLAVERY, THE THIRTEENTH AMENDMENT

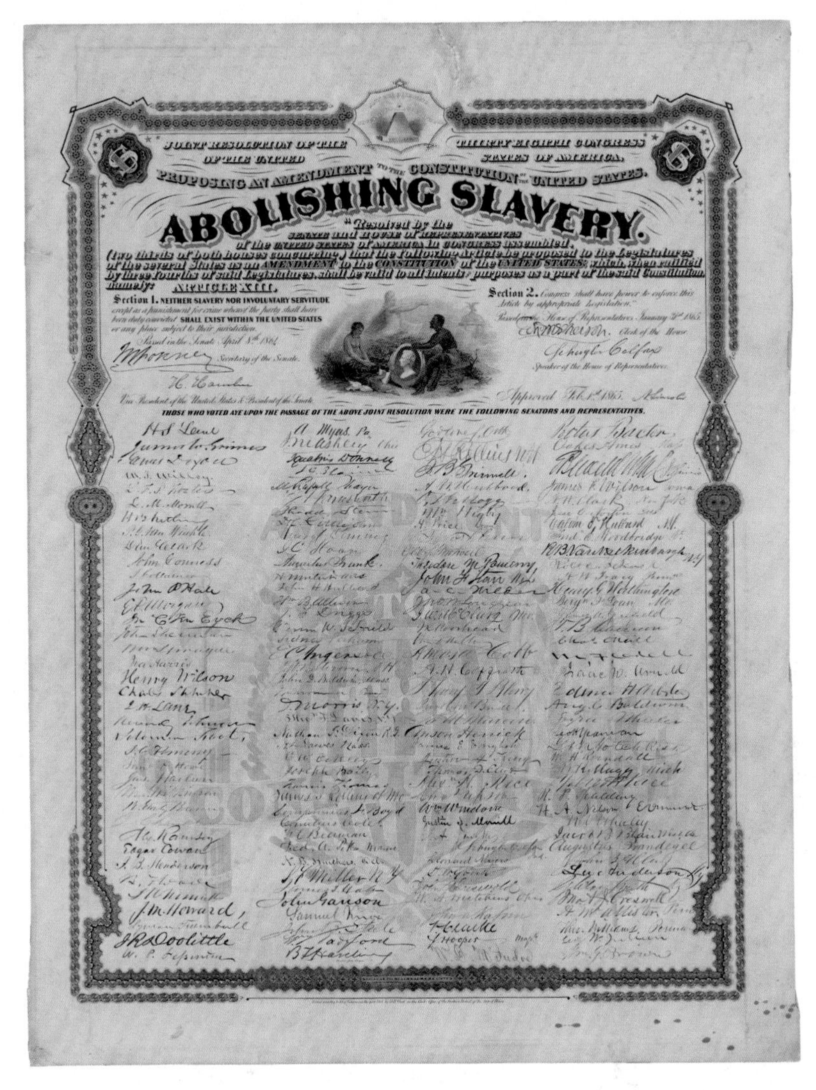

JOINT RESOLUTION OF THE THIRTY EIGHTH CONGRESS OF THE UNITED STATES OF AMERICA,

PROPOSING AN AMENDMENT TO THE CONSTITUTION OF THE UNITED STATES,

ABOLISHING SLAVERY.

"Resolved by the SENATE and HOUSE of REPRESENTATIVES of the UNITED STATES of AMERICA in CONGRESS assembled, (two thirds of both houses concurring,) that the following Article be proposed to the Legislatures of the several States as an AMENDMENT to the CONSTITUTION of the UNITED STATES; which, when ratified by three fourths of said Legislatures, shall be valid to all intents & purposes as a part of the said Constitution, namely: ARTICLE XIII.

Section 1. NEITHER SLAVERY NOR INVOLUNTARY SERVITUDE except as a punishment for crime whereof the party shall have been duly convicted SHALL EXIST WITHIN THE UNITED STATES or any place subject to their jurisdiction.

Section 2. Congress shall have power to enforce this Article by appropriate Legislation."

Passed in the Senate April 8th 1864.

Secretary of the Senate.

H. Hamlin

Vice President of the United States & President of the Senate.

Passed in the House of Representatives January 31st 1865.

Clerk of the House.

Schuyler Colfax

Speaker of the House of Representatives.

Approved Feb. 1st 1865. A. Lincoln

THOSE WHO VOTED AYE UPON THE PASSAGE OF THE ABOVE JOINT RESOLUTION WERE THE FOLLOWING SENATORS AND REPRESENTATIVES.

Passed by Congress on January 31, 1865, and ratified on December 6, 1865, the Thirteenth Amendment was added to the Constitution to effectively abolish slavery, unless "as a punishment for a crime whereof the party shall have been duly convicted." Slavery could thus exist in the country in a different form, with imprisoned people providing free labor.

THE STATUE OF LIBERTY

The 151-foot world-renowned Statue of Liberty, symbolizing the idea of American freedom, was erected in 1886. Though hard to find, placed around the monument's feet are broken chains, a symbolic and painful reminder of slavery in the United States.

NINETEENTH-CENTURY AFRICAN AMERICAN LEADERS

Portraits of Blanche K. Bruce, Frederick Douglass, and Hiram Revels. Bruce and Revels were the only two African Americans to serve as United States senators, both of Mississippi, in the nineteenth century.

NAACP FLAG FLIES IN 1920

In 1920, as part of an antilynching campaign, the NAACP began displaying this flag from the headquarters windows each time a lynching occurred.

MARCH ON WASHINGTON, 1963

Protestors at the March on Washington, August 28, 1963. Around 250,000 people participated in the march, which was one of the largest political rallies in United States history. The event took place exactly eight years after the death of Emmett Till.

Marchers in Washington, DC, seen along the Lincoln Memorial Reflecting Pool of the National Mall

BAYARD RUSTIN

Civil rights leader Bayard Rustin attending a news briefing on the March on Washington, 1963

TONI MORRISON

Author Toni Morrison photographed here at her home in upstate New York. Morrison's parents were a part of the Great Migration, eventually moving from the South to Ohio.

BLACK LIVES MATTER MEMORIAL

Signs at a Black Lives Matter memorial in Washington, DC, commemorate the lives of Black people who have been killed by police, including George Floyd, Breonna Taylor, Oscar Grant, and Tamir Rice.

But minstrel shows had their outspoken critics, among them famous abolitionist, orator, and author Frederick Douglass. A once enslaved man, he described white minstrel performers as "filthy scum" who had "stolen from us a complexion denied to them by nature, in which to make money, and pander to the corrupt taste of their white fellow citizens."

After the Civil War and the end of slavery, Black entertainers appeared in what were still called minstrel shows. The tone of the performances shifted somewhat considering that African Americans were now inhabiting roles that were supposed to be depicting their communities. Still, the same dehumanizing tropes remained in the shows. Black performers were forced to continue to grapple with many of the stereotypes that had been previously established by white performers. Despite the changing times and the federal government's recognition that slavery was wrong, paying white audiences still wanted to see certain types of shows with certain types of tropes.

Minstrel shows would give way to vaudeville- and burlesque-type performances, which would eventually serve as public platforms for new musical genres. Ernest Hogan and Scott Joplin, for example, helped to create the musical genre ragtime in the late 1800s and early 1900s, which would further evolve into jazz. As America headed more deeply into the next century, blues greats like Ma Rainey and Bessie Smith moved to the artistic forefront along with early jazz legends like Jelly Roll Morton, King Oliver, Louis Armstrong, and Fats Waller, among many others.

WHAT'S THAT WORD?

A ***trope*** is an idea that is overused and unoriginal, meaning it's not particularly fresh or forward-thinking. A trope is also quite often untrue. African Americans being seen as servants or buffoons were common Hollywood tropes for most of the twentieth century.

Yet the stereotypes of the minstrel era would still affect other forms of popular entertainment and determine how Black people could present themselves as entertainers. This was the case with Stepin Fetchit, the alias of Florida-born actor Lincoln Perry. Making his first film appearance in 1927, he made it big in America relying on skits such as one where he played "the laziest man in the world." He was also considered the country's first Black movie star.

A CLOSER LOOK: THE HARLEM RENAISSANCE AND *SHUFFLE ALONG*

The ***Harlem Renaissance*** was an African American cultural movement that occurred from around 1918 to 1937. Though Harlem was arguably the center of the movement, the Renaissance's influence was global. Shaped by the Great Migration, Black people from all walks of life produced literature, visual art, music, and theatrical performances that defied narrow depictions of Black people created by the white gaze. Some of the stars of the Renaissance included writers Langston Hughes and Zora Neale Hurston, sculptor Augusta Savage, and prominent intellectual Alain Locke, among many others.

The Renaissance was well underway when musicians Eubie Blake and Noble Sissle's musical *Shuffle Along* debuted in 1921, which made history by being the first Broadway show to have an all-Black creative team. According to Professor Jeffrey C. Stewart, Pulitzer Prize–winning author of *The New Negro: The Life of Alain Locke*, the musical was a source of controversy, with some Black leaders preferring more serious dramas based on Anglo-European ideals.

"*Shuffle Along* is really critical because in many ways the intellectuals like Locke and W. E. B. Du Bois wouldn't necessarily want to go see *Shuffle Along.* They want to go see *Emperor Jones* by Eugene O'Neill . . . a modern psychological drama," said Stewart in an exclusive interview for True History. "In terms of the theater, what's revolutionary is the way in which Black people transformed the stage into this incredible performance that is not seen anywhere else in the world. We're constantly in the position of trying to go in there and extract what we need for an authentic Black representation while keeping at bay the racist cover of it."

Sure enough, *Shuffle Along* had problematic components connected to minstrelsy, with Black actors appearing in blackface for instance. And so-called chorus girls all had lighter skin. Yet, Stewart and other scholars agree that the musical had a profound influence on the stage, helping to create the template for musicals as we currently know them.

"*Shuffle Along* is this incredible repackaging. It's modernism. It's taking something that is somewhat racist and antiquated of the nineteenth century and proposing it as American modernism," Stewart continued, referring to creative expressions that break from the past, offering fresh ways of seeing the world. "And it's so powerful that it becomes the basis of American musical theater. If you go to Broadway now and you go to a musical, the musical is composed like *Shuffle Along*. There'll be somebody who sings, there'll be somebody who dances, then there'll be a lover's spat . . . That whole kind of collage."

III. Blockbusters with Prejudice

By the 1920s, long-form movies were becoming one of America's favorite entertainment pursuits, leading into what would be considered Hollywood's golden age in the '30s and '40s. One of the first notable long-form films was D. W. Griffith's 1915 work *The Birth of a Nation*. Remember when we mentioned this film in Chapter 2, linked to the second rise of the hate group known as the KKK? This virulently racist movie was the first Hollywood blockbuster and continued to be shown into the 1920s. The film gave rise to the lies that a terrorist group like the KKK should be seen as noble, with Black people portrayed as villainous—a willful reversal of the social terror that African Americans had been enduring.

Another disturbing component of the film was the depiction of Black men as predators who sexually assault white women. According to Professor David Pilgrim, this was an example of a common trope: Black men were portrayed as fearsome "brutes," which was used as the rationale for all sorts of real-world violence, including lynching.

NOW LET'S TAKE A MOMENT . . .

Black men being falsely stereotyped as "brutes" in movies . . . can you think of the connection to previous ideas we've discussed in the book? In Chapter 3, we talked about the Central Park Exonerated Five and how they were presented as "savages" in the media. This concept of Black males being dangerous helped to inform the language used for a group of boys presumed guilty of a crime.

Because of the outcry from some surrounding *The Birth of a Nation*'s release, "brute"-type roles for Black men disappeared, with more subservient roles becoming the norm, as seen with Stepin Fetchit. In fact, Hollywood would generally only offer roles to Black people in which they were subservient to white characters, portraying maids, other types of servants, and the enslaved. As it's easy to imagine, African American life was far more varied and nuanced than this. Even amid social obstacles, some Black people were educators, social activists, entrepreneurs, and scientists as seen with luminaries like Carter G. Woodson, Mary McLeod Bethune, Madam C. J. Walker, and George Washington Carver. But Hollywood creators did not deem these types of people as having stories worthy of the screen. African Americans who pursued careers as actors with the big studios had limited options.

A primary example of this phenomenon is seen with 1939's *Gone with the Wind*, which many film experts have recently reassessed, calling attention to its many problems. *Gone with the Wind* was a juggernaut: The four-hour movie ran for four years in theaters and ultimately sold more than two hundred million tickets. In dollars adjusted for inflation—or adjusted gross, which is when you figure out how much money a movie would make in today's dollars—it is considered the top earning film of all time.

And yet the dynamics of the movie highlight many of the concepts we've dealt with in this book. The film, based on a Pulitzer Prize–winning book by Margaret Mitchell, takes place at a big mansion on a plantation, or labor camp, with enslaved people. The story follows the life of Scarlett O'Hara, a Southern woman whose family runs the camp. The story is told from Scarlett's perspective, looking at her romantic drama with a man named Rhett Butler and how she suffers through the Civil War, the glorious days of mansion life fading. And the viewer is encouraged to root for her.

Yet this is a character who at one point slaps a frightened enslaved woman and casually deals with African Americans who are supposed to be content with their enslavement—something we know to be historically untrue. The most prominent Black character in the film is Mammy, portrayed by actress Hattie McDaniel. Mammy is positioned as Scarlett's loyal servant with no life of her own. The character, based on a preexisting stereotype, would become such an iconic figure that the word "Mammy" was used for years after to reinforce certain tropes around Black women. The Oscar-winning script doesn't explore that the woman played by McDaniel might long to be free and have dreams of her own, exactly like Scarlett.

Gone with the Wind was a monumental hit watched by tens of millions more than seventy years after the end of the Civil War, sympathizing with the *loser* of the conflict who had benefited from slavery. It greatly influenced how Black people were perceived in the general culture, especially as other screen alternatives like TV and online streaming services weren't yet available. Individual African Americans and groups like the NAACP protested the film's opening in various cities, reacting with horror at its depiction of Black people.

McDaniel herself wasn't able to attend the premiere of the movie in Atlanta, Georgia, due to Jim Crow policies. In fact, when she won the supporting actress Oscar in 1940 for her role, the first Black woman to receive the trophy, she was sitting in a segregated area apart from white actors. As we mentioned earlier in the chapter, McDaniel had to walk from the back of the room to accept her award. Some people back then regarded this moment as an accomplishment and believed that she should have been grateful for the recognition.

The actress and singer had a prolific film career, though she also played servants in many other roles. Her ability to get work declined as the NAACP continued to protest the subservient parts Hollywood saved for Black people. McDaniel thought the issue was layered, that servant characters could still convey defiance and nuance. In real life, McDaniel had earned enough money to have a home in the wealthy Sugar Hill neighborhood in Los Angeles. Yet this reality—the successes and complexities of her life as an actress divorced four times—was not shown on the screen.

Other prominent films from the time that featured distorted depictions of the once enslaved included Walt Disney's *Song of the South*. The 1946 film, which once again featured McDaniel as a servant, was a fusion of animation and live action and set during Reconstruction. (We spoke a bit about this time period in Chapter 2.) Among other stereotypes that harkened back to minstrel shows, the character of Uncle Remus seemed to yearn for the days of slavery. Like *Gone with the Wind*, African Americans protested the movie's release.

IV. An Important Indie Filmmaker

During this era, the work of Oscar Micheaux served as a counterpoint to massive releases like *Gone with the Wind*. Micheaux was an African American independent filmmaker who released dozens of movies between 1919 and 1948 that were shown in Black communities. An independent, or "indie," filmmaker is one who works outside the Hollywood studio system. Micheaux's screen debut, *The Homesteader*, adapted from a book he wrote, was the first movie created with an all-Black cast. His films were refreshing in that they showcased African Americans with careers as physicians, businesspeople, educators, and detectives, among other non-servant positions. Micheaux's work also dealt head-on with issues like racism, colorism (which in this case refers to prejudice by lighter-skinned Black people toward darker-skinned people), and the criminal justice system. The filmmaker couldn't compete financially with the big studio distribution systems from Hollywood, which then affected how many people could see his work.

Even when Hollywood put forth films with Black actors where they weren't featured as servants or buffoons, Jim Crow still shaped how a movie was made and its final cut. Lena Horne was a famous singer and actress who starred onscreen in Black musicals like *Cabin in the Sky* and *Stormy Weather*. She also refused to play servant roles in predominantly white films. Because she was a wonderful vocalist, Horne was able to appear in several MGM movies during the 1940s that had musical interludes. But her parts were filmed in a way that she could be cut out of the movie for white Southern audiences. And she didn't really interact with other actors on set. As she once remarked in a famous quote, "I became a butterfly pinned to a column singing away in Movieland." Jim Crow made itself known onscreen and offscreen.

V. A Wider Variety of Roles

Performers like Dorothy Dandridge and Harry Belafonte, the stars of *Carmen Jones*, helped to push the idea of what roles were appropriate for Black people. But it wouldn't be until the 1960s when more revolutionary depictions hit the big and small screens. The collective action of African Americans during the civil rights movement caused massive shifts in how we were seen onscreen.

Sidney Poitier became an Oscar-winning movie actor known for taking on lead roles that were groundbreaking during the '60s, both speaking to his craftsmanship as an actor and the changing times. Television—which also had a history of placing Black people in subservient roles as the medium gained popularity in the 1940s—began to reflect the changing times as well. New types of roles opened up. Cicely Tyson, a beautiful model with natural hair who would live to be ninety-six years old, was an elegant costar of the mid-1960s series *East Side/West Side*. The drama told stories of inner-city life. Greg Morris played a tech wizard secret agent in the popular spy show *Mission: Impossible*. Nichelle Nichols portrayed futuristic communications officer Lieutenant Uhura on a massive space vessel in *Star Trek*. (Dr. Martin

Luther King Jr. beseeched Nichols to stay on the show when she was thinking of leaving, because her character was such an important role model.) And Diahann Carroll starred as a witty, stylish nurse and mom on the sitcom *Julia*, which debuted in 1968.

Going into the next decade, *Soul Train* embraced the "Black Is Beautiful" mantra. The TV series, which first aired nationally in 1971, was hosted by Don Cornelius. It featured performances from popular R&B artists and a sea of dancers enjoying one another's energy, movement, and style. And the 1977 miniseries *Roots* garnered massive, record-breaking viewership by featuring depictions of the enslaved in a far more realistic way than had ever been broadcast before on TV. Just a generation prior, such shows would have been unheard of.

Even with these accomplishments, the influence of Hollywood tropes and stereotypes remained. Creator Norman Lear was credited with bringing the African American shows *Sanford and Son*, *Good Times*, and *The Jeffersons* to television. Yet some critics have pointed out that the shows also put forth the same stereotypes that were used to enforce Jim Crow decades ago. These series featured Black people who were no longer seen solely as servants but who sometimes acted in ways that were considered exaggerated and over the top. In the case of *Good Times*, Esther Rolle and John Amos, who played the parents of a family in urban Chicago, were angry that their characters' oldest son had become the show's most popular character partially due to his clownish behavior. And the family seemed destined to be stuck in the ghetto season after season no matter how hard they tried to get out.

Over the following decades, movie and TV depictions continued to morph and transform. Blaxploitation movies marked the 1970s, whereas a variety of Black gangster films and romantic comedies were released from the 1990s into the 2000s. And throughout the decades, there were films about the enslavement of Black people, much more accurate than something like *Gone with the Wind* but still raising questions for many about the types of roles available to Black actors.

On TV, the 1980s had ratings juggernauts like *The Cosby Show* and *A Different World*. The 1990s would offer a range of shows that included sitcoms like *Living Single*, *Family Matters*, *Martin*, *In Living Color*, and *The Fresh Prince of Bel-Air*. And the new millennium had *Girlfriends*, *The Bernie Mac Show*, and *That's So Raven*. Amid all of this, African American characters were seen in a wide range of other shows and movies, though they were still mostly supporting characters who could be killed off at any point during the story. And quite noticeably, even after the civil rights movement and radical changes in opportunities for performers, African American brutes and servants continued to appear regularly onscreen.

VI. From Behind the Scenes to the Screens

Fast-forward to now, the streaming service era, when a wider variety of TV series or films with Black casts are finally getting the green light. Some examples, starting in 2016:

1. A boy in Florida quietly comes to terms with his sexuality while dealing with a mother addicted to drugs. (The Academy Award–winning film *Moonlight*)

2. Over the Christmas holidays, a girl genius tries to connect with her grumpy, isolated grandfather, whose toy shop holds technological marvels. (The film *Jingle Jangle: A Christmas Journey*)

3. A California educator and activist juggles career aspirations, intense romantic dramas, and bodacious friends. (The TV series *Insecure*)

4. A leader of the civil rights organization the Black

Panthers strives to help others while being betrayed by a member of his own group. (The film *Judas and the Black Messiah*)

5. A young, queer woman puts on a winged cape and mask to swing high and vanquish evildoers. (The TV series *Batwoman*)

And Black people wield power behind the camera as well, as seen earlier with Ryan Coogler. Starting in the 1980s, Spike Lee has made more than two dozen feature films, including *Do the Right Thing* and *Da 5 Bloods*, that reflect the lives of African American audiences while provoking critical discussion. In 1991, indie director Julie Dash released the acclaimed drama *Daughters of the Dust*, which would serve as a major influence for Beyoncé's visual album *Lemonade* more than twenty years later. In the new millennium, directors and screenwriters Ava DuVernay and Tyler Perry produced contrasting types of work that have become must-see viewing for an array of fans, with Perry owning his own studio. And a Black woman show creator—Shonda Rhimes—has become known for producing hit after hit for TV with casts of characters from different backgrounds.

Yet the legacy of old Hollywood has persisted. Online protests like #OscarsSoWhite—a reaction to all the actors nominated for Oscars in 2015 and 2016 being white—recognize previous decades in which legions of entertainers were shut out of the system. Many people knew the history and wanted to point out how aspects of Jim Crow have continued. The protests also highlight that many people find the Oscars to be behind the times, that the awards don't matter as much to people who have many more viewing options compared to decades ago.

A CLOSER LOOK: AVA DUVERNAY'S ARRAY

We've talked about representation onscreen in this chapter, but representation behind the scenes is important as well. According to the 2021 Hollywood Diversity Report, great strides were made with diverse onscreen representation but representation behind the scenes is still pretty low. That same year, director, screenwriter, and producer **Ava DuVernay** started a database called Array Crew. This database provides opportunities for women and people of color to work as crew on film and TV sets. Highlighted jobs range from assistant directors to photographers to barbers. DuVernay's efforts are part of a movement recognizing the importance of representation in all aspects of the movie production process. Initiatives like this provide a professional path for many people who've been shut out of an industry long dominated by white men.

DuVernay is known for initiating change. For instance, she employed all women directors for her TV series *Queen Sugar.* "I mean, I think when we think about diversity and inclusion, we have to go beyond just declaring it," she said about her efforts with Array. "I said a couple of years ago I was not going to do any more panels or articles about diversity. I was going to create tools to make sure that people could actually practice it, and so this is the outcome of that thinking."

Oscar-nominated movies like *The Help* (2011) and *Green Book* (2018) have also been criticized because, for some, they continue the tradition of old Hollywood films we discussed. Black people are again seen as servants or their lives are secondary to white figures. *Green Book*, which focused more on the white racist character than the African American musician he was chauffeuring, won the 2019 Oscar for Best Picture. Though *Green Book* was lauded for its performances, many critics thought it was stuck in the past. Some would have preferred *Black Panther* to win, even if they weren't superhero fans. This was because the movie featured Black characters whose experiences were completely centered.

In fact, many critics were happier about the success of the film that won for Best Animated Feature. This movie earned more than $375 million around the world and tells the story of a Brooklyn Afro-Latinx student developing special powers because of a radioactive bite from an arachnid. As he does so, he learns how to be present for himself, his family, and the world.

The person in question? That would be Miles Morales, whom some of you may know as the oh-so-smart star of *Spider-Man: Into the Spider-Verse.* He's a teenager with a big heart on a multidimensional journey. And he is at the center of his own story, showing us all how to be a hero.

LET'S TALK ABOUT IT

* What connections can you make between the minstrel shows of the nineteenth century and some of the Hollywood movies we talked about from the twentieth century? Why do you think white people enjoyed watching minstrel shows?

* Do you feel like Hattie McDaniel's Oscar win should have been celebrated back in the 1940s? Or still be celebrated now? Why or why not?

* What TV shows or films have you watched where Black or brown people are centered in the story, where they're not only supporting characters? Out of these films or shows, do you have a favorite? Why? Please explain in detail what you appreciate about this movie or show.

EPILOGUE

This book has focused on providing many details on how a system of legal oppression has shaped the contours of the United States for generations in ways that might be surprising to some readers. And though measures were enacted to end things like segregation and redlining, it would be a big mistake to assume that the policies of Jim Crow are a thing of the past. The legacy of Jim Crow still actively shapes how and where people live, how citizens are policed, and how communities are presented on the screen.

For example, as mentioned in the book's introduction, new voting restrictions have been put into place in states like Arizona, Florida, Georgia, and Texas[1]. Some members

---

1."Map: See Which States Have Restricted Voter Access, And Which States Have Expanded It," NPR, last modified September 7, 2021, https://www.npr.org/2021/08/13/1026588142/map-see-which-states-have-restricted-voter-access-and-which-states-have-expanded.

of the media have called these new measures a type of "Jim Crow 2.0." The reason this term has arisen again is that such voting restrictions imply that those who've historically *not* had political power, including African American citizens, will have new obstacles to face when trying to vote. Other states have, in contrast, expanded access to voting for their residents, but certain key states like Florida and Georgia now decide presidential elections, making access to voting in these regions a top priority to maintain democracy.

Even as the legacy of Jim Crow continues to impact lives, there are leaders who persevere, who strive to create a fairer, more equitable land. Stacey Abrams, after conceding the Georgia governor's race in 2018, went on to organize and spur thousands of people to turn out in record numbers at the polls during the 2020 elections. This culminated in the state electing a Democratic president—the first time this had happened since 1992—and electing two Democratic senators who became the first Black and first Jewish senators for the state. (She did all of this while maintaining her career as a writer of romance novels and a political thriller!) Pulitzer Prize winner Annette Gordon-Reed explored the legacy of Juneteenth in an acclaimed historical text and memoir released in 2021, the same year that Juneteenth became a national holiday. Scholar Jelani Cobb has reintroduced to the world the Kerner Commission in his 2021 book that explores the implications of the commission's findings for our world today. (Remember how we discussed the commission in Chapter 3, where we focused on policing and prisons?) And R&B singer/songwriter/musician H.E.R. has chronicled aspects of the African American experience in sociopolitical songs like "I Can't Breathe," "Fight for You," and "Change," receiving Grammy and Academy Awards for her efforts.

As we chronicle systems of oppression, it's important to recognize those who have pushed back while living and thriving and celebrating their place on this planet. The front of this book eloquently depicts such modes of existence. Artist extraordinaire Steffi Walthall has crafted a cover featuring a series of mostly old-school television sets (some readers might be peering at these boxes like, "What are those?") depicting key scenes from the civil rights movement. We see scenes of those who pushed to eradicate Jim Crow, lifted from the many nonviolent marches that were pivotal in effecting change, while also seeing glimpses of those who were arrested for their activism. She's also created an image of a burning bus that would have belonged to the Freedom Riders. These were groups of activists who were testing anti-segregation laws when their bus was firebombed in Anniston, Alabama, on Mother's Day 1961. (Congressman John Lewis was in fact an original Freedom Rider.)

But the TV screens also feature those who managed to defy Jim Crow in other ways by creating wondrous art and reshaping the world of entertainment. The bottom left screen offers a portrait of Cicely Tyson, an actor who earned an array of accolades over the course of her ninety-six years on this planet in film projects like *Sounder* and *A Hero Ain't Nothin' but a Sandwich*, television projects like *The Autobiography of Miss Jane Pittman* and *The Women of Brewster Place*, and stage projects like *Tiger Tiger Burning Bright* and *The Trip to Bountiful*. On the screen at the bottom right, we see the music group the Supremes, who were at the forefront of the Motown sound of the 1960s with sparkling verve and Detroit glamour. The trio would end up having a record-breaking twelve No. 1 hits and twenty Top 10 hits on the Billboard pop charts. The Supremes' songs were generally apolitical. Still, they proved that Black artists were not only capable of occupying airwave space during times of rampant oppression but could readily dominate. Going forward, lead singer Diana Ross went on to release her self-titled debut album in 1970; the record was mostly written and produced by couple Nick Ashford and Valerie Simpson, serving as a masterpiece of symphonic soul-pop.

Amid the struggle against unjust policies, these stories must be recognized and serve as the template in which we see ourselves, informing who we know ourselves to be.

It's from this place we shall proceed.

RECOMMENDED MEDIA

A huge amount of work has been released over the years that connects in some way to the history and legacy of Jim Crow policies. Here's a tiny sampling. I wanted to be sure to present a mix of books, films, and TV shows to speak to different people's tastes. Works have been categorized by whether they would be considered nonfiction or fiction, though some of the fiction projects are very much informed by real-world events, as seen with the film *Selma*, for example. It's my hope that the explorations of these projects will feel rich and fruitful to a variety of readers.

WORKS OF NONFICTION

Greenfield-Sanders, Timothy, director. ***Toni Morrison: The Pieces I Am***. Magnolia Pictures, 2019. https://www.youtube.com/watch?v=BtWdy8pFktM.

An exploration of the literary legacy of Nobel Prize–winning author Toni Morrison, including her nuanced, transcendent perspectives on race, community, and the creative process as a writer.

Kates, Nancy, and Bennett Singer, directors. ***Brother Outsider: The Life of Bayard Rustin***. San Francisco: California Newsreel, 2002. DVD.

A look at the life of the pacifist and civil rights activist who was the primary organizer of the 1963 March on Washington, among many other accomplishments. Rustin was openly gay, and the film describes the ways in which he navigated homophobia during a more broadly conservative era.

Lewis, John, Andrew Aydin, and Nate Powell. ***March***. 3 volumes. Marietta, GA: Top Shelf Productions, 2013–2016.

As told by the late Congressman John Lewis, who represented Georgia in the House of Representatives for more than thirty years, this trilogy of graphic novels depicts key, pivotal moments from his early life and leadership in the civil rights moment in captivating detail.

Peck, Raoul, director. ***I Am Not Your Negro***. Magnolia Pictures, 2016. https://www.netflix.com/watch/80144402.

This Oscar-nominated work chronicles the realities of American structural racism, including Jim Crow, through the writings and speeches of author James Baldwin, with narration by Samuel L. Jackson.

Wilkerson, Isabel. ***Caste: The Origins of Our Discontents***. New York: Random House, 2020.

As chronicled by award-winning journalist Wilkerson, a deep, historical dive into the ways in which an entrenched, rigid racial caste system has shaped the United States of America.

Wilkerson, Isabel. ***The Warmth of Other Suns: The Epic Story of America's Great Migration***. New York: Random House, 2010.

Wilkerson provides a magnificent overview of the Great Migration while focusing on the lives of three African American citizens who relocated to different parts of the United States during the mid-twentieth century.

WORKS OF FICTION

Butler, Octavia E. ***Kindred***. Garden City, NY: Doubleday, 1979.

A revered sci-fi/fantasy book where the main character, Dana, is transported back in time and space from 1970s California to Maryland in the 1800s. She is then forced to live as an enslaved woman while looking out for her abusive white ancestor, who's initially a child. A provocative examination of the grim, horrifying realities of slavery.

DuVernay, Ava, director. ***Selma***. Paramount Pictures, 2014. https://www.youtube.com/watch?v=Abkka8Vf2_M.

A look at the personal and public struggles of Dr. Martin Luther King Jr. and Coretta Scott King during their efforts to end the Jim Crow policies that imposed unjust voting restrictions on African Americans. The movie zooms in on the importance of the marches that took place in the city of Selma, Alabama, leading to the Voting Rights Act of 1965. Considered the first biopic for the big screen with King as the lead character.

Hansberry, Lorraine. ***A Raisin in the Sun: A Drama in Three Acts***. New York: Random House, 1959.

This drama depicts the plight of a conflicted African American family with plans to move into a predominantly white neighborhood despite an association's plot to keep them from relocating. The play, which was also adapted into a 1961 theatrical film and a 2008 TV movie, was inspired by Hansberry's own family experiences.

Larsen, Nella. ***Passing***. New York: Alfred A. Knopf, 1929.

A trailblazing work published during the Harlem Renaissance where a light-skinned woman of African descent decides that she will escape persecution by passing as white, entering into marriage with a hateful, racist man. The novel was later adapted and released as a Netflix film in 2021.

Lindelof, Damon, creator. ***Watchmen***. Aired 2019 on HBO. https://www.amazon.com/Watchmen-Season-1/dp/B07RGXX891.

This sprawling, Emmy Award–winning TV series partially follows the life of a youngster who survived the Tulsa Massacre of 1921, as well as his relationship to an African American police detective who's adopted the costumed identity Sister Night. The epic show plays with real-world history in a variety of ways while depicting the intergenerational impact of trauma.

(Special note: The themes and sensibilities of *Watchmen* are very mature and generally inappropriate for younger viewers. The series is geared toward older teens and adults. Parental discretion is advised.)

Morrison, Toni. ***A Mercy***. New York: Alfred A. Knopf, 2008.

In this sparse page-turner of a book, Morrison focuses on the life of a young enslaved woman in the late 1600s, during the time of America's early colonial settlements. The story deftly explores themes of loss, yearning, possession, and freedom.

ACKNOWLEDGMENTS

First and foremost, I'd like to give my utmost thanks to Janet Hill Talbert, my former boss and mentor at Doubleday Broadway, who provided the opportunity for me to enter the book publishing industry. Janet, it's been a blessing not only to work together but also to have you as a role model. You've shown me how to perennially infuse insight, respect, and kindness into what you do while being a top-notch pro. The time spent working with the highly esteemed Christian Nwachukwu Jr. . . . priceless. Eternal gratitude, my friend.

As I've learned firsthand over the years, even though many people direct their attention to individual authors, books are in fact a highly collaborative process. Thus there is a team of people behind the crafting of this book who should be acknowledged as the supreme professionals that they are. To Nicholas Magliato, thank you so much, wondrous gentleman editor, for the thoughtfulness with which you've guided and shaped this work, especially considering the amount of moving parts there were to contend with. Tyiana Combs, your sharp insight and enthusiasm as the manuscript took shape, so invaluable and thoroughly appreciated. And Jennifer Sabin, thank you for the opportunity to serve as a contributor to the True History series and providing a captivating platform for a variety of voices.

I'd also like to send hearty, hearty thanks to the Penguin Workshop production team. To Caroline Press and Shona McCarthy, your meticulous eye, depth of knowledge, and powers of organization are spectacular. Additional thanks go to Tess Banta, Sophie Erb, and Lynn Portnoff, with major kudos to artist Steffi Walthall, who splendidly executed the cover concept in a way that mixed real-world history with compelling art.

To Katie Yamasaki, Roland R. Acevedo, and Jeffrey C. Stewart, many thanks for your time and the original interviews you provided for the book. The wisdom each of you continue to impart to the world is invaluable.

To the group of women whom I see as epitomizing

the concept of Black Woman Magic in the industry—Stacey Barney, Melody Guy, Kelli Martin, Rakia Clark, Cherise Fisher, Porscha Burke, Krishan Trotman, Rockelle Henderson, and Gilda Squire, among others—thank you for the inspiration, opportunities, and being such wonderful colleagues.

Outside of the publishing world, to my boys and BFFs Daniel St. Rose and Leroy Bryant, rock on y'all. You've witnessed me go through many stages of personal and professional development, and I'm beyond grateful for your support through the years. Thank you for a beautiful friendship full of nuance, reflection, and zaniness, and for simply allowing me to be me.

To Richard Haynes (smiling . . . do you think we should finally find out if we're related?), thank you, lovely pal, for the continued enthusiasm you've shown for the crafting of this project, for the deep conversations about life and learning, and for facilitating the introduction to the superb David Ikard.

To my family in New York and Florida, including Delfina Ferguson (Tia!), Lu-Anne Rivera, Delia Griffin, Sergio Ferguson, and Nadine Ferguson, thank you for the roots, the cheer, and the love. I must also give heartfelt thanks to my cousin, educator and writer Carmen King, for providing a consistent sense of safety as I grew up and being the first person I can remember who taught me about the beauty found in all types of literature. And I'm beyond grateful for the cherished friendship and support of Kendra Hurley, Sandeep Prasada, Christopher Moore, David Seymour, Erin Cassin, Leah King, Vidal Green, and Olga Grant. Leading lights on this planet, hand to heart.

I must also point out that this book was written primarily in Berlin, Germany. To my divine Deutschland posse: Ute Ledwon, Günter Gebhardt, Christoph Lamptey, Inci German, Mika Nienen, and June Chua, thank you for the genuine support and helping me navigate a new city while handling my business. Special shout-outs as well to Ina Ruehl in Munich, Jakub Kocmánek and Karel Jarusek in Prague, and Charles Aina, Paul Smith, and Merle Joseph in London. I'd especially like to thank my close friends Robert Peters and Jens Rauenbusch for the care and interest you've shown in my publishing projects while serving as consistent (and modest!) examples of excellence. And super-duper shout-out to the great Melody Makeda Ledwon. Melody, your intellectual fierceness, general care, and breadth of knowledge about the Diaspora continue to nourish the soul. Thank you very much. You have a multitude of stories to share.

And finally, most importantly, I want to say thank you to educators and the fabulous young people who've inspired the creation of this book. Your collective openness to new ideas and curiosity about what's *really* come before embolden me to approach so much of what I do with care and integrity. Here's to envisioning a more just, loving world.

ABOUT THE AUTHOR

A native New Yorker, Clarence A. Haynes is an editor, writer, and content manager who has experience in various parts of the publishing industry. Having been trained on the copyediting desk of the newspaper *Newsday*, he worked as an editor with the educational publisher Youth Communication before moving to the book world, where he served as an associate editor with the Doubleday Broadway division of Random House and the imprint Harlem Moon.

He has gone on to work as a developmental editor for dozens of titles with Amazon Publishing under imprints like 47North, which specializes in sci-fi/fantasy, and Skyscape, which specializes in young adult fiction, where he was the editor for the best-selling Hundredth Queen series. Having also written for platforms like Huffington Post and Biography.com, Clarence has continued his copyediting work with a variety of Penguin Workshop titles, including the

Who HQ series, and is the cowriter of a forthcoming Afrofuturistic novel for Delacorte Press. He lives in Brooklyn, New York, and Berlin, Germany. Wherever he goes, he tries his best to surround himself with books.

For more True History, read an excerpt from *The Founders Unmasked*

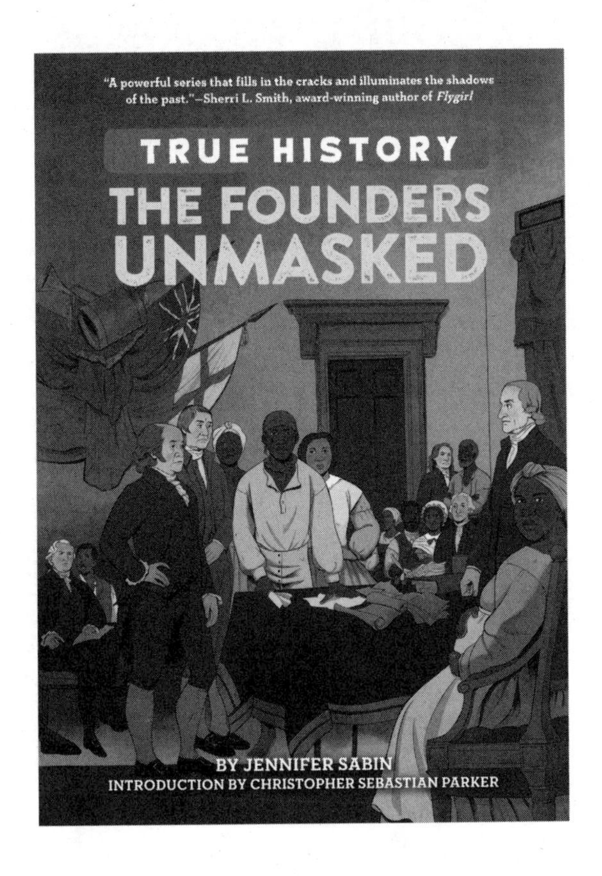

CHAPTER 1
A COUNTRY'S CREED

When Thomas Jefferson arrived in Philadelphia in 1776 for the most important summer of his life, he wasn't alone. A fourteen-year-old named Robert Hemings traveled with him from Virginia to the city where thirty-three-year-old Jefferson would write, and sign, the Declaration of Independence. Hemings was a body servant, or valet, to the Virginia plantation owner and future third president of the United States. He helped Jefferson dress and shave. He ran small errands for him. He followed him when he rode horseback and likely brought him his meals. He had no choice but to do whatever he was told: Hemings was one of the many Black people Jefferson enslaved. He was also the half brother of his wife.

While Jefferson drafted one of the most famous documents in US history, Hemings waited on him hand and foot. Maybe it was Hemings who refilled Jefferson's inkwell as he wrote the lofty words of that great document, which declared Americans free from British rule and free to pursue their dreams: "All men are created equal."

Robert Hemings, however, wasn't free to pursue his dreams. Neither were hundreds of thousands of enslaved Africans living in the colonies at the time. As the Patriots fought and died for their freedom from Great Britain and the rule of King George III, they continued to deny freedom to enslaved Africans.

HISTORY RECAP

Colonists were the settlers in British America. ***Patriots*** were the colonists who fought the British for their freedom. ***Loyalists*** supported the British cause and did not want to break from Great Britain.

Jefferson wasn't the only slaveholder in Philadelphia

for the momentous meeting of the Second Continental Congress that summer. In fact, the majority of the fifty-six men who signed the Declaration of Independence enslaved Black men, women, and children at the time. Some of the men enslaved several servants to work in their homes; others enslaved hundreds of people to work their plantations, (now called labor camps by some), build their houses, cook for their families, and take care of their personal needs. Two of the more famous delegates in attendance were Benjamin Franklin of Pennsylvania and John Hancock of Massachusetts, both now known as Founding Fathers. They each enslaved several people. John Adams, also from Massachusetts, was there for the signing, too. Adams, who would become the second president of the United States, was one of the only Founders to never enslave Africans.

HISTORY RECAP

The **Declaration of Independence** was written to permanently break ties with Great Britain. Though war had broken out a year earlier with the Battles of Lexington and Concord, the document officially declared war against the British Empire and explained why it was necessary. It was also created to persuade colonists who weren't so sure they wanted to break from Great Britain to back the cause for independence. And it was meant to help the colonies request aid from foreign governments.

The Declaration was adopted by the **Second Continental Congress**, meeting in Philadelphia, that was made up of delegates (representatives) from all thirteen colonies. Think of it as the United States' earliest form of national government. The First Continental Congress took place in 1774; the Second Continental Congress operated from 1775–1781.

Some of the most important men in this period of US history were not Declaration signers, but they're generally referred to as Founding Fathers for their critical roles in the formation of the United States. Included in this group are Alexander Hamilton, future secretary of the Treasury of the United States; James Madison, future fourth president of the United States; and, of course, George Washington, commander of the Continental Army fighting the British, and the future first president of the United States. These men enslaved people as well, although the story of Hamilton is a bit more complicated. (More about Hamilton in Chapter 3.)

The hypocrisy of the signers continuing to enslave people as they demanded their own freedom from British tyranny is not a new idea.

IT'S JUST A NAME, ISN'T IT?

In an exclusive interview with True History, Margaret Kimberley, senior columnist for *Black Agenda Report*, says the term **Founding Fathers** itself is problematic because it affirms patriarchy and white supremacy, and it has been elevated over time.

Patriarchy means a society or system of government run by men that gives women little or no power. ***White supremacy*** is the belief that white people are a superior race, which creates a structure of white domination over people of color and other cultures.

Kimberley says these men were not gods, though we often treat them as if they were. "People always talk about the Founders, the Founding Fathers, and they're deified [worshipped as a god] so you can't change anything in the Constitution . . . It keeps the country frozen in time, frozen in this moment of conquest, in enslavement. By deifying them, you deify what they did."

In this book, they are referred to simply as Founders and mostly leave *Fathers* behind.

Your teachers may have talked to you about viewing the lives of the men who shaped the nation in the context of the historical period. If we look at them through that lens, they certainly weren't the only slaveholders in 1776. That same year, enslaved Africans comprised around 20 percent of the population of the thirteen colonies and as much as 40 percent of the southern colonies. Slavery was permissible by law and was common, even in the northern colonies. It was a key to wealth and power, particularly in the South. And the Founders were men of wealth and power. They were elite patriarchs of a society governed by the belief in white supremacy.

Even as early as 1776, there were colonists advocating for the emancipation of enslaved people. For example, the Quakers, a religious group, opposed slavery. And just one year later, in 1777, Vermont became the first colony to ban slavery. But don't be fooled. This wasn't a very common point of view.

WHAT'S THAT WORD?

Emancipation is the process of setting free people who are enslaved. President Abraham Lincoln issued the

Emancipation Proclamation in 1863, declaring all people enslaved in the United States to be free. That was nearly one hundred years after the Declaration of Independence was written.

In this context, it might not be surprising that so many of these men owned slaves. What might be more surprising is to consider what some of those men actually thought of slavery. What did they believe should happen to the men, women, and children they enslaved? Did they think they should be freed? And how did their writings, public statements, and actions contradict the very words they wrote: "We hold these truths to be self-evident, that all men are created equal, that they are endowed by their Creator with certain unalienable rights, that among these are life, liberty and the pursuit of happiness."

And what did each Founder do, or fail to do, to end slavery?

II. A Declaration for Some

Leading up to the signing of the Declaration of Independence, some of the Founders wrote or spoke about the horrors of the slave trade. So why then didn't they include a plan to end slavery in the document?

In a testament to the power of editing, Jefferson wrote a clause attacking Great Britain's King George III that was ultimately left out of the Declaration of Independence. If it had been included, the country's relationship with slavery might have ended sooner—although that is up for debate.

> [H]e has waged cruel war against human nature itself, violating it's [sic] most sacred rights of life & liberty in the persons of a distant people who never offended him, captivating & carrying them into slavery in another hemisphere, or to incur miserable death in their transportation thither. [T]his piratical warfare, the opprobrium of infidel powers, is the warfare of the CHRISTIAN king of Great Britain. [D]etermined to keep open a market where MEN should be bought & sold, he has prostituted his negative for suppressing every legislative attempt to prohibit or restrain this execrable commerce: and that this assemblage of horrors might want no fact of distinguished die, he is now exciting those very people to rise in arms among us, and to purchase that liberty of which he has deprived them, & murdering the people upon whom he has obtruded them; thus paying off former crimes committed again the liberties of one people, with crimes which he urges them to commit against the lives of another.

Clearly, there's a lot to unpack here. *Opprobrium? Execrable commerce? Obtruded?* Let's look past the old-school language and break it all down from a modern perspective.

In the final version of the Declaration of Independence,

there are twenty-seven grievances—or complaints—specifically against Great Britain's King George III. These are all the reasons the Patriots wanted to be free of British rule.

HISTORY RECAP

The colonists wanted to be able to write their own laws and create their own representative government. The king was tightening his control over all aspects of the colonies: their rights, their economies, and their legal systems. They wanted to be free of those controls, what they called the ***tyranny*** (cruel and oppressive government rule) of the king. The last five grievances attack King George III for waging war on them.

Jefferson's omitted grievance has two important parts: The first accuses the king of inflicting the evil of slavery on the colonists and keeping it alive through the slave trade, as if against the colonists' will. Fact check: That was false. Nobody was forcing colonists to enslave people. The truth is, like so many other plantation owners, Jefferson was dependent on slavery. In fact, America's growing economy relied on the institution of slavery.